THE WOUNDED PILGRIM

THE DARK UNCERTAINTY

GW00503407

THE DARK UNCERTAINTY

WRESTLING WITH SUFFERING
AND DEATH

Sarah and David Clark

DARTON · LONGMAN + TODD

First published in 1993 by
Darton Longman and Todd Ltd
1 Spencer Court
140–142 Wandsworth High Street
London SW18 4JJ

ISBN 0–232–51976–5

A catalogue record for this book is available from the British Library

Phototypeset in 10½/12½pt Bembo by Intype, London
Printed and bound in Great Britain
at the University Press, Cambridge

CONTENTS

FOREWORD

The 'Wounded Pilgrim' series is inspired by the belief that spiritual growth demands an openness to experience and a willingness to accept the challenge of self-knowledge despite the suffering, confusion and agony of spirit which this can involve.

In different ways each book attempts to focus on the brokenness of the spiritual pilgrim and to face those areas of pain and struggle which are all too frequently swept under the carpet by the institutional churches or to which simplistic or dogmatic answers are given. The hope is that such books, written by those who do not flinch from the exploration of personal suffering and who acknowledge the complexity of social and psychological reality, will touch the hearts and minds of those who yearn for nourishment on their spiritual pilgrimage but who find the life of the Churches hard to bear, or who have long since abandoned the practice of institutional religion. The series is also a passionate response to the Churches' call for a decade of evangelism or evangelization. It reflects, however, a deep antipathy to the spirit of crusading and triumphalism and to the tone of theological and moral certitude which not infrequently characterize evangelistic campaigns.

The authors in this series write from the perspective of those who have no glib answers. They share a common determination to be true to themselves and to the reality which they experience. In short, they are courageous seekers who write in the hope that their own honesty will offer strength and a sense of companionship to those who have perhaps been deeply hurt by life's events and not least by the judgementalism of what sometimes passes for spiritual guidance.

BRIAN THORNE

PREFACE

HOW WE WROTE THIS BOOK

Our experiences are very different: our inner experiencing has been very different. Sarah says that my life would be seen as outwardly very much more adventurous than hers; and I would say that her life could be seen as inwardly more adventurous than mine. We work in different ways, and so we have decided to take separate sections of this book, according to our own experience. Each section in the list of Contents is initialled to indicate the writer.

Some parts of chapters and their postscripts were first published as articles for parish magazines. Chapter 9 on Tears began life as a paper delivered to the Ecumenical Society of the Blessed Virgin Mary, was first published in *One in Christ* (report of the Seventh International Congress of the society, 1986), then in *Mary and the Churches* (Columba Press, 1987), edited by Alberic Stacpoole OSB, and has been supplemented.

Many people have had a hand in shaping the material for this book and we are very grateful to all of them. We should like especially to thank all those who have worked with us as clients and parishioners, and whose stories (very often altered considerably to protect identity) have informed the pages of this book. I am grateful to my colleagues in our parish for their patience with me during the writing of the book, and to Christine Tippin, parish secretary. We are grateful to Jim Cotter, Alison Greenwood, Jacky Whall, Henry Evans, Allan O'Leary, Fran Walsh, Bill Kirkpatrick, Pat Fitzsimons, Judith Smith, Sarah Woodard, Oliver Bernard, Alan Webster, Chris Roberts, Dick Jones and others who have kindly read various chapters and given helpful advice; though the final work with its views

ix

remains ours alone. We should like to thank our editor, Brian Thorne, for encouraging us, especially when we thought it was all too difficult.

DAVID AND SARAH CLARK
Petertide 1992
Oadby, Leicestershire

ACKNOWLEDGEMENTS

We are grateful to the following for permission to quote copyright material: Patric Dickinson from his *A Rift in Time*; Five Seasons Press from *Five Peace Poems* by Oliver Bernard; David Higham Associates from 'The Ballad of the Bread Man' in *Collected Poems* by Charles Causley published by Macmillan; H. J. Richards from his *God's Diary* published by Columba Press, Dublin.

And in the garden secretly
And on the cross on high,
Should teach his brethren, and inspire
To suffer and to die.
  JOHN HENRY NEWMAN, *The Dream of Gerontius*

Father, give us we pray
the faithfulness to endure
the dark uncertainty.

BISHOP JOHN TAYLOR

INTRODUCTION

WRESTLING WITH SUFFERING AND DEATH

Then Jacob went on his journey, and came to the land of the east. (*Genesis 29:1*)

Jacob went on his way and the angels of God met him; and when Jacob saw them he said, 'This is God's army!' (*Genesis 32:1*)

And Jacob was left alone; and a man wrestled with him until the breaking of the day. When the man saw that he did not prevail against Jacob, he touched the hollow of his thigh; and Jacob's thigh was put out of joint as he wrestled with him. Then he said, 'Let me go, for the day is breaking'. But Jacob said, 'I will not let go, unless you bless me'. And he said to him 'What is your name?' And he said 'Jacob'. Then he said 'your name shall be no more called Jacob, but Israel, for you have striven with God and with men and have prevailed'.[1]

Jacob is one of the archetypal wounded pilgrims. Not only a pilgrim outwardly, travelling widely in the Middle East, but an inward pilgrim, coming to terms with his fear of his twin brother, Esau (the hairy man!) and learning to cope with the stupidity of his over-zealous sons. Perhaps the most famous of the incidents associated with Jacob/Israel is this strange story of his wrestling with the angel. It speaks of the mystical struggle with God and the inner self. It suggests that such a struggle is a lonely one, undertaken in the dark. And so it seems to me:

1

wrestling with suffering and death is no less than a struggle with God and the inner self. Jacob here is the archetypal struggling human being, determined to hang on to the mysterious stranger: 'I will not let you go, unless you bless me!' So, wounded with a dislocated hip, he is blessed and given an additional name, Israel (which means 'Ruling with God').

Being blessed through struggle with God and humankind, being blessed through wrestling with pain and death may seem perverse to the western hedonist mind. But it is profoundly true in human experience. We learn, we grow, we hurt, we are wounded; we can be blessed through the struggle.

The Church, as heir to the Judaeo-Christian tradition, claims to have a deep understanding of both suffering and death, and yet the image it often projects has an air of superficiality. Fatalistic clichés abound: 'It is the will of God' (what kind of God is that!); 'She bore her suffering manfully (sic)'; 'I always felt that Jesus was close' (what of those faithful Christians who feel a great emptiness?).

We want this to be a book of real experience, facing both those whose suffering (and death) seems to be surrounded with the light of God's presence, or transcendent awareness, and those whose journey takes them to the lowest depths. We shall hope to convey the sense that those who are suffering may find help from those very people who, through their struggles and anguish, have found help themselves.

I am convinced that it is a fundamentally Christian view that new life often emerges from the most unpromising material, but I also see that Church people so often (in a very human way) sweep under the carpet those aspects of life, and the life of Christians, which speak of vulnerability and brokenness and guilt. I find, however, that when the 'heavier' and most difficult areas of life are tackled, sometimes underneath the darkness you find the richest colours.

I remember from twenty-five years ago, a gruelling three hours visiting the patients in the wards of a 'cottage' hospital in Lancashire. I was a young curate, discovering the pain and suffering of some people with cancer and unnamed conditions which made them smelly and hard to approach. Yet I received from these people such a sense of love and courage that as I walked home, reflecting on what I had heard and seen, I was overtaken by an exaltation of spirit, a rare surge of deep joy: often it seems that God shows us that the most Christlike attitudes and behaviour are in people who are either on the fringes of or completely outside the Church's life.

Everyone has an initiation into suffering and death. My first close encounter with death was as a young teacher, aged twenty-one, in Nigeria in 1960 and it made a deep impression.

A 'mammy-wagon', that is, a jerry-built bus, careered into the ditch with a burst offside front tyre. With characteristic lack of concern for safety, the man who hired the vehicle had been standing on the driver's running board. The vehicle had fallen on him. When I arrived on the scene, the passengers, mostly women going to market, were lamenting and wailing, with their hands on their heads. No one seemed to have a clue what to do. I went to the injured man lying on the road in the hot sun. His chest and shoulder were laid open and I thought he could not live. He was lifted into the back of my battered A40 Countryman, and held down by two helpers. I drove as fast as I could to the hospital, which was seventeen miles away, praying fiercely that he would survive. He died halfway there, and I delivered a corpse.

Two things stand out of this experience for me: first, that still wet behind the ears and suddenly initiated into the inevitability of death, I received no sympathy or support from the staff of the hospital on arrival. Looking back, I wonder if this was because in Nigeria death is not as hidden as it is in this country. The hospital staff may not have imagined that this was a new experience for me. The second was that the orderlies who put the dead man on a metal trolley misjudged the edge of the footpath and tipped him into a flower bed. This violent death and the lack of basic care and respect for a dead body shocked me deeply.

Fortunately, I had time to brood on the incident, to feel my feelings and to write about it all in long letters home. I did not know why I had become so involved; I did not know the man who died. He was acting recklessly in any case. The bystanders and other passengers had behaved helplessly. But I had instinctively taken action, and found within myself an urge to save

3

this man's life at all costs. Then afterwards, I was angry with the carelessness and the off-hand attitude of the hospital staff. Later, I discovered Donne's famous words, written on his sick-bed,

> No man is an Iland intire of itself; every man is a peece of the Continent a part of the maine; if a Clod bee washed away by the Sea, Europe is the less . . . Any man's death diminishes me because I am involved with Mankinde.[2]

Now I know why singing these words in Priaulx Rainier's setting is so powerful.[3]

This initiation into death, sudden death, was scant preparation for the next contact with death which I experienced in a personal way when I was twenty-eight. That was the death of my father from cancer at the relatively young age of fifty-seven. There were some messy aspects of that dying and death which give substance to my claim that the Church (and of course I mean its lay members as well as the clergy) projects an image of superficiality, while pretending to due solemnity and care. This often results in an additional death: the death of feeling, or at best a distortion and diversion of feelings.

In the mid sixties, I had read articles in the *Church Times* which moved me, about the value of openness and honesty in facing death. It seemed that where people could acknowledge their forthcoming death and talk about their fears and hopes openly, there could be a healing of the spirit. It was suggested that where relatives could weep together, they would then be able to face the end with fortitude, knowing of the love that existed between them.

With me, none of that was possible. Because it would take away hope, my father 'must not know he was dying'. I bet he did anyway: he wasn't stupid, though of course it may be that he needed to deny the facts, and that this was his strategy for coping. My visits were infrequent, because we lived a long way away, and each time I resolved during the journey to tell him the truth, which would allow us to talk honestly together. Each time on arrival, I felt constrained. Did he really want to know he had an inoperable cancer of the pancreas? At the end he did know because it blew up like a football, but by then he wasn't talking much. I felt terrible looking at him.

Then I became cool, in control, being 'helpful' to mother and the family. I was persuaded that the stiff upper lip was what was required; or I colluded with the messages that the rest of the family sent out. I cannot remember what was said at the funeral, but it was all very proper.

It was not until ten years later, in a counselling session, that I wept openly for my father. For twenty minutes. And my feelings for him and my love of him, my gratitude for him, began to surface again. It was only after that outburst that I became frequently aware of his influence, especially at times of spiritual happiness and exultation.

I relate this story to show how easy it is to learn to suppress the feelings that would in other cultures normally accompany the loss of a beloved person. It is common, and it is tragic. It is tragic because this is the very way in which we may find healing from the pain of our loss, and the dying person, if he wishes, may alleviate the loneliness of dying. The Nigerian women at the road accident wailed and wept, giving physical expression to their grief in the postures of their bodies. God seems to have made us in such a way that, if we can acknowledge our deepest feelings and emotions and give them expression, we find relief from the pain.

While saying this, I know that for some people this in itself would be too painful. There is no universal formula. We each have to discover the path that is right for us.

This book is about wrestling with the twin phenomena of suffering and death. We recognize that in order to find relief from the crippling effects of suffering, we shall have to wrestle with ourselves and with others. My experience is that personal and spiritual growth occurs when we wrestle with conflicts within ourselves. If we are fortunate, someone who loves us may join in on the side of the angels.

I went through one of those kind of struggles during a training course at Ammerdown near Bath. It was a five-day course on understanding how small groups work, run by the Church of England's Board of Education. The atmosphere was emotionally highly charged, because we had been invited to live and be with personal authenticity. Often, the groups had no task but to observe their own behaviour, and how people interacted: who dominated, how alliances were made, and what the group achieved by being together. Also, we played games – games in which we were enabled to discover, sometimes to our discomfort, sometimes to our delight, what kind of a person we really were. I remember tackling all this at the beginning from an intellectual point of view, not acknowledging what I was feeling.

A crisis arose in which I became aware that I was refusing to look inside myself. It felt as if my inner feelings were altogether too dangerous to let out, that I might see the fearful temper that I had displayed as a small boy. Everyone who has limited or even killed their feelings has a very good reason for having done so: usually to protect themselves from what they imagine – again, often with good reason – will be very painful, or because they have been taught to fear their feelings. Sadly, this is very common in British society.

But then, in the sunshine and freedom of Ammerdown, a centre dedicated to spiritual growth, I found myself in a battle for my soul. On the one side was my internalized, protective control over feelings, taught by parents from the best of motives. On the other was my desire to become a more integrated person, adventuring into the unknown. The latter movement was encouraged, no, being cheered on urgently by Sarah. I felt that a great carapace was in place, over a dangerously turbulent purple sea of feelings. The carapace developed a crack, and I saw the richness of the possibility of an interior life with all the emotions of which I was capable. The tears of fear and horror gave way to tears of relief.

This formative experience began an unravelling which has enabled me gradually to become more at ease with myself, and therefore more available to others as a multifaceted human being. The experience of violent death, duly absorbed and accepted as a young man; the private and personal undergoing of the loss of father; the recovery of feelings which had been suppressed and buried – if all these essentially painful experiences were to be of ultimately positive use, then appropriate reflection was essential.

In the chapters that follow, we shall describe some of the wounded pilgrims with whom we have had the good fortune to travel, sometimes only briefly, sometimes for a longer period. My overall impression of the journey is as a kaleidoscope of harrowing beauty: the sword that pierces the heart, like the anguished sunlight of Schubert's last piano sonata, the totality of Bach's Passion music, or the Michelangelo *Pietà*.

The beauty is related to the transcendence of God. The postscript to this introduction is provided by Sarah, and is to an extent inspired by an antipathy we share for the trivializing influences which seem to bedevil parts of the Church's life today.

POSTSCRIPT

'If there is a God, I am quite sure he is the sort of God who doesn't mind whether you believe in him or not.' This was a gentle rebuff by a much respected cathedral Dean to my small-fry panic about the integrity of having my baby baptized when doubts seemed to be consuming my faith. It was a great relief.

> In the beginning was the Word and the Word was with God and the Word was God. He was in the beginning with God; all things were made through him, and without him was not anything made that was made. In him was life, and the life was the light of men. The light shines in the darkness, and the darkness has not overcome it. (John 1: 1–5)

The light, however tiny, is never extinguished: it shines through the banality, through the blandness and the anodyne material with which it is swathed; it shines through the horror and the cruelty. Through the occasional parting in the clouds there are shafts of splendour momentarily revealing the possibilities of all the clarity and the truth that there are: the immense power and energy and mystery of love.

Some years ago when things seemed to be falling apart at the seams for us, with marital difficulties, mental turmoil and an impasse in communication, we came across a poet's clear-cut distilled arrogance, voicing the shallowness of finding solutions to the vast mysteriousness of living.

TWO SORTS

There are the surface people
Who pause and eat time with you;
And the living-underneath
Who can tell you, if you ask,
About spaces the surface-people
Won't dare to bury you in,
For fear it might disturb
The spin of their flat earth.[4]

When the mystery is taken away and everything is bathed in certainty, I find myself flattened and discouraged by what seems to be a debasing of the currency of experiencing. There is a part of me which says that rationality cannot explain everything, that faith cannot be made to carry everything; there has to be room for doubt. There is a shadow side. I am human, I have potentials for both positive and negative. I have within me, as we all have, the capability of loving and the capability of destructive evil. Parts of me I know and recognize, parts of me I do not know yet, and parts of me I shall never reach. There is for me a never-ending exploration until maybe, at the very end, I shall know even as also I am known.

If prayer is valid, it is something to do with the unknowableness of God. Prayer is something to do with wrestling with the impossible, wrestling with the majesty, the terror, the awe, the mystery, the pain, the fear, the infinite tenderness, the grandeur, the humour, the humility which is God – and the total absence of this. It is the search for the unknowable. It is the struggle to understand that which is ever mysterious and for ever held in the tension of paradox. It is to do with that which is unattainable; it is that perfection which contains within it all that is imperfect.

Most of the time, in the earth-bound practicalities of jobs, work, people – eating breakfast, arguing, computing arrangements – there is little space for transcendence.

When I was a young woman the news reached us of another young woman, a friend of the family, who had died with her infant in childbirth. It was tragic and shocking. But to me it was also an event full of awe. Within myself, I heard this phrase: 'She's done it; she's achieved it.' I do not understand this even now, but it is still around: a feeling that death is a huge and terrifying challenge.

I began my working life with young children in playgroups and teaching, then moved to work with adults and marriages. Now in middle age, I work with people who are dying and with the bereaved. There is for me a sense of something appropriate and right about this. I do not think I could have arrived at this position any earlier, but I have a sense, nevertheless, of being in the right place for this particular stage of my pilgrimage, whatever that may mean.

Kierkegaard wrote 'Life must be understood backwards . . . but it must be lived forwards', according to a quotation in a rather remarkable cookery book,[5] and it seems that at certain times there are opportunities of surveying the view from a new vantage point.

Occasionally there is vision. Occasionally there is a glimpse of beyond. I climbed a mountain. It was one of that range which Bunyan called the celestial mountains. I was alone with all the company of heaven. The peace I experienced in that rare air, where the view was breathtaking, in that tiny fragment of time within eternity, was a peace so profound that I would have been totally unable to conceive it in my imagination.

It is that peace, with its 'maximum of fruitfulness'[6] that I search for. It is excruciatingly difficult to find its elusive pulse, in the very complex ambiguities involved in husbanding the resources of which I seem to be the centre – my own resources and those of the people I love. There has to be a culling and destroying as well as a rhythm of continual inspiration and expiring. There is a ruthlessness as well as a loving and profound tenderness.

God is there in the joy and the peace, and God is there in the pain, the struggle, the dying and in the bereavement. I do not understand it; it is far beyond the scope of my human imaginings. But with the encouragement and help of fellow wounded pilgrims, I can go on searching and see that the light is still shining in the darkness.

1

ONLY CONNECT

Early on a Sunday morning, when the light was still in that soft, pearly blue transition between dawn and clear daylight, a huge, luminous, full white moon hung low and motionless, as if in suspension, over the houses at the top of the street. An elderly gentleman walking to church jerked his thumb in the direction of the vast, tranquil orb, and remarked, 'We're pretty insignificant, aren't we?'

Insignificant little earth-bound creatures we are, in such a comparison, yet we have connections with the mysterious moon. Throughout the ages people of different religions and philosophies have found in the moon a symbol of new birth which rises to a consummation and then fades; the moon's waxing and waning have been felt to be deeply significant. In his book, *The Night of the New Moon*,[1] Laurens van der Post, who was held as a prisoner of the Japanese, wrote:

> Even now, after all these years [nearly a quarter of a century after the ending of World War Two] I, who know little about astrology, am not a follower of astrologers, and who have no wish to make an astrological point of any kind at all, feel compelled to say that it looked at the very least most strange to me that the first atom bomb dropped by man should have been dropped on so moon-swung a people as the Japanese, during the phase of nothingness between the death of the oldest and the birth of the newest of new moons . . .
>
> It is to me almost as if, out of the depths of life and time . . . some cosmic impulse had come to extinguish the

moon on this occasion so that its extinction and imminent rebirth could act on the limited awareness of man as an unmistakable symbol of annunciation that the past was dead and a new, greater phase of meaning about to begin on earth, however catastrophic the introduction.

Probably we shall never know exactly what part that new moon played in the suffering and in the ending of suffering during the final stages of World War Two, but there is no doubt that the complexity and interconnectedness within the whole universe is immense and mysterious. Primitive cultures realized the earth's dependence upon our sun for heat and light and for life itself. We have known for centuries of the magnetic drawing power of the phases of the moon upon the ebbing and flowing of the tides of the seas. Only in more recent times have we become aware of the complexity of the ecology of the earth and begun to realize the interconnectedness of courses of action, and non-action, in our world.

When the rain forests are felled for timber the results are felt acutely and immediately by the indigenous population there. Eventually, the effects reverberate throughout the whole world; thus the decimating of the forests of the Nepalese foothills has become a major source of the calamitous floods in Bangladesh, hundreds of miles away. Rivers and seas all over the world are polluted with waste; soil is eroded causing deserts to expand. Acid rain caused by toxic gases and industrial waste damages the trees of countries far beyond the frontiers of the developed nations whose factories produce the pollution. Chloro-fluoro-carbons (CFCs) from the industrially developed world damage the fragile shield of the ozone layer in the atmosphere surrounding the earth, which screens us from the harmful effects of ultra-violet radiation. This thinning of the ozone layer has world-wide repercussions not confined to the areas where the CFCs are used. The first 'ozone hole' was discovered opening up over Antarctica, and there was evidence of another 'ozone hole' over the Arctic; the results of these holes is damage to crops and ocean food chains, as well as a great increase in the incidence of eye and skin diseases in both people and animals.

The list of the links between action in one part of the world and suffering in another is endless.

The media, that great connector of both people and events, can bring us satellite pictures of test matches on the other side of the world, and can show us the Olympic Games, and the reactions to election results everywhere. We can watch the royal weddings, and treat ourselves to the light relief of comic shows or following the soap operas, or we can find our recreation in concerts and masterclasses; but we are also given coverage of the wars and violence in different parts of the world, and in our sitting-rooms we can see starkly and vividly the plight of refugees from both war and famine. Television connects us with all we might like to have or be and it can also connect us with all who have no opportunities. It connects us with entertainment and delight and also reveals the huge uncrossable gulf between that idealized life and the life where there are no such luxuries. Grey, concrete tower blocks in vandalized surroundings, with the daily menace of muggings offer no encouragement to self-esteem and creativity – nor does the harsh glitter of the bright smart shops displaying goods which are out of reach for those who are caught in the poverty trap.

On the steps leading up to the grandly designed architecture of St Pancras Station there are the young men wearily asking the apparently insignificant but scandalous question of the passengers rushing by: 'Have you any spare change?' Huddled in the well-lit shop doorways of Lincolns Inn Fields there are the blanketed figures, curled up against the cold. They are some of the people who have given up the normal routes of finding a niche in the fast-moving lanes of modern living, who reveal the connection between lack of concern, lack of affirmation, lack of love and resulting alienation.

The advertisements on the television, in the profusion of newspapers and magazines, and on the hoardings squeezed into every spare space on every available corner, are trying to lure us into believing that success means owning and consuming and that these will provide the route to desirable power. In his book *Walk to Jerusalem*,[2] Gerard Hughes wrote:

The enemy in capitalist countries is not communism: the

enemy in communist countries is not capitalism. We have a common enemy: whatever can stifle or kill the human spirit. The affluent society in which the accumulation of wealth and status are accepted as the higher good, is much more effective in crushing the human spirit than death squads and torturers. Once the human spirit – the spirit of love, of compassion, and tenderness – is stifled then Lucifer can take his ease, because his minions will do his work for him, and to protect their wealth and their status they will destroy not only themselves, but all life on earth.

Gerard Hughes, like Laurens van der Post, perceives that evil and violence are not out there, beyond, found only in others; the connections are within us, within our own minds. Van der Post, reflecting upon the problems of evil, writes:

> Villains undoubtedly do exist . . . but they do so in a mysterious and significant state of interdependence with the profoundest failures and inadequacies in ourselves and our attitudes to life . . . as if the villain without is a Siamese twin of all that is wrong within ourselves.[3]

It is more comfortable to believe that violence, cruelty and prejudice are outside and not inside. I recall the horror which I felt as I found myself seething with violence towards my five-month-old baby who would not stop crying. I realized how fortunate we were – the baby and I – that another adult walked in at that point, because there was scarcely a paper-thin membrane between me and baby battering. Baby battering is not confined to families described as 'underprivileged' and 'inadequate'.

It takes courage to stand out against the values dominant in our society. There is the East Anglian poet who silently witnessed to the urgent need for disarmament, wearing billboards outside the cathedral in Norwich one whole day every week for years. He is a remarkably gentle man, yet determined to bring before the public his choices in life. Thus he lives simply and commits himself to Christian CND as joint Chairperson. His 'Visit to London', the beginning of which is given below, is a gently ironic account of his night in the cells after a demonstration:

> CHARGE SHEET. On Wednesday 22nd February 1984 at Bridge Street S.W.1. you did without lawful authority or excuse wilfully obstruct the free passage along the highway. *Con Sec 137(1) Highways Act 1980*
> On Wednesday 22 Feb 1984 wilfully obstructing Steven West a Constable of the Metropolitan Police Force in the execution of his duty. *Con Sec 51(3) Police Act 1964*

The theology for this afternoon
Is, as usual, love.
Not abstract love to faceless multitudes,
But love that is always there to do, like work;
And can't be done enough of, can't be finished.
And much as I'm loved,
(And I must be, look at the pavement under my feet,
Look at the railings standing reliable,
The sky lighting my life),
I can't give enough for others; I can only
Give what I can. At least I can today.

This afternoon at two o'clock love locks
Thirteen of us to the House of Commons railings,
Unfolding banners posters pieces of paper
Saying the arms race is a violation
Of international law and of conventions
Agreed by various governments including
Our own. And I am here with the other twelve
Because my government is breaking
Higher laws than these.
I mean Christ's laws for the workers of the world
And for those who imagine they're working it.
All I lost was my chains and one of the padlocks:
The police kept them, I didn't have time to claim them.[4]

The ethos of the way lives are being lived around us has its effects. How I live affects who I am, because of the interconnectedness of body, mind and spirit. This is something which is made horrifyingly clear in a study by Professor Eugene Provenzo, entitled *Computer Kids*.[5] Professor Provenzo's findings about these computer games are that they foster sexism, racism and violence, which perhaps comes as no surprise in our increasingly disturbed world. But it is an uncomfortable insight that these games may be adding to the accumulation of suffering because those who watch and play indiscriminately will be dulling their senses against the real effects of violence. The players may fail to realize the interconnectedness between what they are doing and the effects upon themselves and society. After all, 'it's only a game'.

> The world of Nintendo [computer games] and video games in general, is one of violence and mayhem, populated by prize fighters, terrorists, SWAT teams . . . People do not realise that the computer is not neutral, but in fact channels us and frames our view of the world . . . There are no conscientious objectors in the world of computer games.

Our beautiful, fragile earth has so much to offer us, in its astonishing richness of natural resources, and in the amazing achievements which are possible with co-operation and generosity, yet often there is so much alienation and competitiveness in the face of threat that the inevitable consequence is suffering. In our society the expectations which predominate seem to be about living in health with as much wealth as can be amassed. Those without wealth are frequently rejected as of little consequence, and feel themselves pushed out to the fringes, as we see in the chapter about the Norwich Night Shelter (chapter 5). There we shall read about the women and men who staff it. Theirs is a difficult task, working with people who cannot comply with ordinary expectations and values. The staff has to do battle with respectable society, because their clients are not respectable and do not conform: we, the respectable, may prefer not to see our own vulnerability mirrored in the disreputable. Those who are not bothered about the state of the bank balance, but who struggle for peace in anti-nuclear causes, or for justice or for ecological issues may also be looked at askance by the neighbours. Those who suffer disease often feel out of step with the marching forward that the rest of society keeps up. Those who are dying, whose bodies are breaking down in irreversible decay may feel very lonely in this health-conscious age, where the finiteness of each human being is kept at bay for as long as possible. The fear of AIDS is but one aspect of this.

Mental illness too still carries stigma, a stigma of which I was made poignantly aware by a woman who knew she had lost her way. She knew her normal threads were broken for the time being and that she was sinking into some fearful terror; but she could remember sufficiently the reactions of society – or perhaps it was her own fears – to those who had been inside 'loony bins'. She jittered with horror: 'They'll all look at me and point their fingers.' In despair she wailed that it would be different if she were ill in a surgical ward rather than a ward of a psychiatric hospital. She feared she would never be able to look people in the eye as an equal again.

The stigma strikes insidiously. Even in the nineteen-nineties, even in the caring professions, there are schools of thought still prevailing in which to give way to human emotion is to be considered weak and to be eyed with suspicion, viewed as 'wimpish', branded as 'unstable'. Such behaviour may be punished by lack of a reference or by ostracism.

Perhaps it is the fear of the brilliant clarity of creativity that drives totalitarian regimes to imprison sane dissidents with strong drugs in psychiatric institutions, as well as trying to break them down with psychological and physical harassment and deprivation. And perhaps the stigma is to do with the very fine dividing line between normality and abnormality, even where abnormality encompasses genius.

In such ways human beings inflict punishment and suffering on one another, causing hurt because non-conformity appears to be a threat to the smooth running of the system. But there are other ways of perceiving. The mystical view is revealed by Iulia de Beausobre in her book *Creative Suffering*.[6] She is writing of the *Yurodivy*, the 'born fool', not a person viewed with awe because of his utterances, not a person of stature in society, but one whom we have all met and then maybe looked away from in embarrassment, as we do not quite know how to respond to the vacant eyes or the dribbling mouth or the ingenuous smile.

> From a practical point of view, no useful purpose is served by anything that the *yurodivy* does. He achieves nothing. Yet there must be some strong attraction at work to draw men (and women too), poor creatures most of them, to choose such a rough and comfortless life, manhandled from time to time, pelted by children and set on by dogs . . . The aim of the *yurodivy* is to participate in evil through suffering. He makes of this his life's work, because, to the Russian, good and evil are, here on earth, inextricably bound up together. This is, to us, the great mystery of life on earth. Where evil is at its most intense, there too must be the greatest good.[7]

Not only the *yurodivy* in Russia but people around us, too, reveal the strange links between suffering and the true joy of life. I am not thinking of 'the noble army of martyrs' but of men and women who live everyday ordinary lives, yet whose understanding of situations seems to lead on to a different track. I read recently of a man with a harelip and a cleft palate whose speech was difficult to understand at first. His gifted wife had died young after a miscarriage, leaving him with three young children.

> 'I have thought a lot about him,' [since his death] the author of the article, Patrick Nuttgens wrote, 'about living at the least possible expense . . . about the joy of life in everyday things. I asked him one night if he had a good definition of happiness. No, he answered, he had not. But he had a good definition of unhappiness. 'Unhappiness', he said, 'is the refusal to suffer.' He was the happiest friend I ever made.

Miss H. was one of the most serene friends I ever made. She was a gentle, diminutive, unassuming, retired teacher-trainer. She had lived through two world wars, and learnt much about loss as well as acquiring a gentle wisdom in the process. She stuck to her belief about being able to teach a mentally handicapped boy regarded as ineducable. Miss H. and the boy took a liking to each other, and some twenty years later, when we met them, the young man of twenty-five could not only read and write, albeit in elementary fashion, he could escort her, now aged over eighty, across the road and help her on to a bus. Miss H. took all this as a matter of course, believing and hoping both in herself and the boy, but she had had to ignore all those who scoffed at her and were ready with ridicule for the handicapped child.

Her accepting attitude to all those with whom she came in contact was recognized by a tough lorry driver. He had managed to hold down a job and marry, but now that his children were learning to read, he was embarrassed and afraid that his illiteracy would attract their scorn. Miss H.'s simple matter-of-factness enabled the lorry driver to pluck up courage to ask her to teach him – very privately – to read. They settled down to the Ladybird Reading Scheme and the *Daily Mirror*, a plan which worked admirably.

Miss H. was a wounded pilgrim who was happy to journey with all kinds of fellow pilgrims. At her funeral I was astonished how many and varied were the friends who came to pay homage to her. She had made connections with so many walks of life, having been one of the first women in this country ever to fly, having kept goats, having loved children and been fascinated with geology, botany, music, poetry. She had certainly lived life very fully. She had, to a very considerable extent, satisfied her need for balance and connection between the intellectual, the emotional, the physical and the spiritual aspects of her being.

Elisabeth Kübler-Ross, the Swiss-American doctor whose work for the dying has now become well known in many countries, refers to these four aspects as 'quadrants'. It is her belief that we need to realize the connections between all four quadrants, and that contemporary life tends particularly to neglect the spiritual quadrant. Undoubtedly, because we are complex creatures, the different aspects intertwine and affect each other. Some people learn to compensate when one part is stricken down. Just as sighted people are often astonished by the degree to which blind people have developed their senses of hearing and touch, and equally that deaf people can become sensitive to vibrations in a way that most hearing people are oblivious to, so, similarly, a person afflicted by loss of physical co-ordination may develop the other quadrants and become wonderfully rich intellectually, emotionally and spiritually. Many people have been awestruck by the mathematical brilliance of Professor Stephen Hawking, now almost totally paralysed by Motor Neurone Disease contracted about thirty years ago. However, because of the vital connections between the quadrants, the damage or neglect to one may have a devastating effect upon the others.

Some years ago there was a series on the television based on the true stories of escape from German prison camps by British prisoners of war. The one I remember most vividly was profoundly moving to me, I think because it illustrated so graphically the holistic nature of the human organism.

In all the stories, the challenge of escape was ever present for the men of the captured British forces. In order to keep defying the enemy all possible and many seemingly fantastic and impossible plans were explored. In this particular episode, the men were discussing the fact that any prisoner who was clinically diagnosed as mentally ill would be returned to Britain; one prisoner volunteered to try this road to freedom by simulating an unbalanced state of mind. He realized that if he were found to be shamming it would have disastrous repercussions not only for him and the other PoWs but particularly for those who were genuinely ill. Thus he arranged with his fellow internees that he would be shunning communications with them from the moment that he began to play out his bleak depression. Following this stricture, he did not dare risk an opportunity of letting go and sharing with even one trusted person what he was experiencing in this lonely enactment of a grey and wretched condition. Day after day his deteriorating spirits were noted and reported; he refused to respond to the attempts to jolly him up as he withdrew more and more, often silently weeping. There was a desolate, poignant moment one morning when he was standing dejectedly amongst the ranks of the men for roll call, and he wet himself.

Eventually he was classed as mentally unfit, and a car came to the camp to fetch him away to be repatriated in England.

His companions were jubilant at the success of the plan, only to be desperately sobered by the letter which was addressed to them, weeks later, by his wife; she thanked them for the care they had shown him and gave them a short bulletin on his mental state – as an in-patient of Ward X in an English psychiatric hospital.

Nearer to home, there was an instance of a similar kind, where the connection between the outside situation and the inner world affected mental stability. A school drama society was putting on Arthur Miller's play *The Crucible*. It is a harrowing work dealing with the witch hunts in seventeenth-century America, when morality seemed to have gone mad; normal decent people were as easily swayed as ever, but even the apparently strong were unable to remain impervious to the forces at work in what was supposed to be a Christian society. Religion was no help; corruption had infiltrated. No one seemed to be untainted by the evil.

One of the cast in this school production, an impressionable and sensitive teenager called Alison, had a small speaking part and she took on the role as the prompter during the rehearsals and for the end-of-term performances; she was thus deeply immersed in the bewildering and sinister atmosphere of the play for many weeks. Her mother, who was unfamiliar with the play and equally ignorant of the historical material on which the play was based, became perturbed at her daughter's anxiety and her unusual lethargy and tearfulness at home, amidst the usual ups and downs of family life. When all the outward events should have added up to excitement in the run-up to the performances, her daughter seemed to be shut up in a peculiarly cheerless outlook on life. Alison was unable to explain her misery; she felt frightened and alone and was unable to attribute these deeply depressing feelings to any particular source.

When her mother came to watch the second performance of the play, during its four-day run, she was struck by the devious and insidious mixture of good and evil, where nothing was clear or clean, where destructiveness prevailed while masquerading as goodness.

End of term meant the end of Alison's role as the prompter, and her natural sunniness reasserted itself. Her mother realized at last what had been undermining her daughter's confidence, how the lack of a clear morality in the play had eaten into her still developing and not yet firmly established sense of herself.

The school drama society was taking the play abroad in an exchange with a school on the Continent. It seemed imperative to her mother that for Alison's well-being she should not be subjected to a second immersion in this confusion of values which had so seeped into her before. She discussed the matter with a teacher, who was astonished at her concern, but it was finally decided that an adult should take on the task of prompting, which allowed Alison to cope easily with her small part and enjoy sampling some of the difference of culture available in another European country.

The effect upon the inner worlds of these two people, the prisoner of war and the teenage schoolgirl, by the parts they were playing and the atmospheres surrounding them, reveals the incredibly delicate balance between the *psyche* and the *soma*: between all the millions of different cells and nerves and the fine networks which connect them all. It is remarkable how the balancing mechanisms adjust to all the various strains and stresses put upon them in day-to-day living; most of the time it all works well. However, so vulnerable and delicate are the checks and balances of our organisms, that it is difficult to remain immune to the influences of our environment, and most of us find ourselves affected by prevailing atmospheres, as well as the situations which impinge upon us.

It can be disquieting to even the bravest soul to feel that events are running out of control. To a tiny infant, whose dependence on others is total, the experience of having no firm constant connection – or bonding – with a mother figure can become almost unendurable.

A ten-week-old boy was transferred to the parents who hoped to adopt him. He had been handled by his natural mother in hospital and had then been fostered by two or three other mothers before the adopting parents took him home ten weeks later. When he was between three and four months old, his adopting mother fed him at lunch time then left him with a baby-sitter for a couple of hours. She returned to look after him, give him his tea-time bottle, bath him and put him to bed with his older brother and sister. Unavoidably, she had to be out in the evening too, and when she came back the baby-sitters said he had never settled. For forty-eight hours she tried to cuddle him and give him the security he needed, while she felt desperately that he was in some way damaged. Something was terribly wrong although she was unable to pinpoint what it was. The baby's cry was apathetic; he woke mechanically to feed, but made no pleasurable noises, would not look at his mother and seemed to have forgotten how to smile. He seemed totally withdrawn.

This very young child was without means of expressing his nightmare fears that he had been abandoned, and certainly at that tender age he had not had the chance to develop the mental and spiritual strength needed to withstand the assaults inflicted upon him by the frequent changes of mothers who cared for him. He needed constancy from his fellow pilgrims even to set out on his journey.

In retrospect his mother understood this, and understood also why he found it so difficult to trust women. For many months after this terrible weekend, he scarcely looked at his mother and was much more quickly comforted by his father when he was experiencing the usual childish distresses.

I think, for that baby, the constancy of his father helped to alleviate the pain of the betrayal he felt women had dealt him. In time, he was able again to look at his mother and eventually to bond with her. But the fear of being abandoned remained inside. He wept desolately when a dog the family had under-taken to look after was left at home while they went out for a couple of hours. Shortly after that, when he was eight years old, his mother, leaving the family with the father, went away for a week-long course. It seemed, by the end of the week, that his whole body was locked in this fear of being abandoned again, and he appeared to be brewing up tonsillitis. On the mother's reunion with the family, he cried wordlessly with her, tears pouring down his cheeks for nearly half an hour, until she whispered 'Did you think I wouldn't come back?' Then the tears ceased and after a little while his face became suffused with transparent joy. The incipient illness disappeared without trace, though he kept very close to his mother for the next few days and he needed to test the strength of her love for many years to come.

Emotional pain bites deeply and none of us enters into adulthood without scars. All of us, in Harry Williams' phrase, 'are emotionally shop-soiled' by the connections and the lack of connections between our needs and the responses of those around us. The experiences of childhood are deeply embedded. However, these experiences are also part of our resources as fellow pilgrims on the journey. Bruno Bettelheim, in recruiting staff for his school for very difficult children, realized that he needed young people to work closely with the pupils, but those who came from happy, secure backgrounds did not have the life experience to relate to these children. He needed young adults who already knew at first hand something about suffering. For some people whose wounds are deep healing may come through love, in relationships; or it may be that the love comes through psychotherapy. Freud, in a letter to Jung, wrote 'Psychoanalysis is in essence a cure through love.' For others it may be that the wounds, covered only by sensitive scar tissue, erupt in adult life when outward events resonate with them (see chapter 8). But whatever responses emerge, there are indelible intertwinings between conscious behaviour and unconscious promptings.

In an extraordinary inner journey, Carl Jung set out to discover more about these intertwinings, these connections with which he had become deeply fascinated in his work with patients. In this journey, he 'consciously submitted himself to the impulses of the unconscious'.[8] Laurens van der Post, who knew Jung well, described this experiential research; he begins his recording of Jung's gigantic 'Dante-esque journey' with these words:

> [It was] one of the bravest decisions, I believe, ever recorded in the history of the human spirit. He committed himself to this equinoxal urge from within [to probe the depths of his own psyche] and in doing so apparently subordinating reason to unreason, and risking the sacrifice even of sanity to insanity . . . His whole spirit must have

reeled with an inverted vertigo and horror of what he was about to do.[9]

This was Jung's voluntary confrontation with the workings of his own unconscious. In his *Memories, Dreams and Reflections* he wrote:

> I hit upon this stream of lava and the heat of its fires reshaped my life. That was the primal stuff which compelled me to work upon it, and my works are a more or less successful endeavour to incorporate this incandescent matter into the contemporary picture of the world.[10]

It seems strange that there can be links between the work of a psychologist delving into the labyrinthine twists of the human psyche in order to understand better the interconnectedness of conscious and unconscious, masculine and feminine, the unique and the general, and the vastness of the universe, in which our planet is but a tiny speck, and *homo sapiens* an even smaller particle upon it. Yet it seems that this is so. Scientists are discovering that the whole universe is engaged in a 'cosmic dance of energy'.[11] They are finding that the new perception of the interconnectedness which has emerged 'raises the intriguing possibility of relating sub-atomic physics to Jungian psychology'. The new discoveries affirm 'the similarities between the views of physicists and mystics'. The connections are endless: between external and internal, conscious and unconscious, physics and mysticism, mathematics and art, body and mind, suffering and pain, pain and joy. We need to realize, in Fritjof Capra's words, 'that good and bad, pleasure and pain, life and death are not absolute experiences belonging to different categories, but are merely two sides of the same reality; extreme parts of a single whole.'

And in the connections lies our hope.

POSTSCRIPT

Should religion and politics mix? Is Christianity political? There are complaints from both politicians and members of the congregation when politics and spirituality are intertwined from the pulpit.

Jesus seems to have been an uncommonly courageous man. Besides being sensitive, compassionate, and having a piercingly keen understanding of the difficulties and dilemmas of life, he was forthright and daring. His message was not muffled by threats from the officers of religion nor those of the state.

He was faced with certain death unless he avoided the confrontation with the authorities whose values and actions he perceived as being in opposition to the creative love of God. The mutterings had begun early on because he connected things in a different way from the usual conventional responses to law and order: he had not upheld the traditional ways of dealing with adultery (John 8:3ff); he dared to overthrow Moses' sacred commandment, 'Thou shalt not . . . on the Sabbath', because it was more important to satisfy hunger and to love and heal (Luke 6:2ff and John 5:2ff). What is more, he encouraged the sturdy independence of the man he had healed. Not only was Jesus in those moments throwing aside hallowed tradition, he was bringing life to people so that they found the courage to uncover latent resources which had lain dormant for years. Love is potent. To those who enjoy the comfort of the familiarity of the religious straitjacket, or closeted Christianity, such love is dangerous.

Jesus the son of Joseph, an insignificant carpenter, was put to death because his living and his loving were a threat to the established order. He feasted with joy and battled with evil. He did not avoid confrontation because all would be well in the Kingdom of Heaven, in the life after death; he was concerned with life and love and wholeness in this world, now. He offered life and exercised love to the fullest extent during his short mortal life on this finite planet earth. He came to bring life and to bring it more abundantly to the blind, the crippled, the ill, the deaf, the poor – and to the rich and comfortable, if they could understand and receive him. Nor was he content to go around 'doing good' in a quiet manner that would excite no trouble, that might ingratiate him with the powers that be. He allowed full play: those who opposed him had plenty of manoeuvering space, and plenty of opportunity to discover their own humanity if they wanted to, and to witness his tears and his grief. The battle for freedom against all that was, and is, in opposition to the uncompromising reality of love, escalated until it reached the highest religious and secular courts in the land, and he was rejected of men. It became expedient that he should die. It was politically more expedient to kill him whose love inspired a dangerous freedom and courage than to punish a notorious murderer. He was well aware of the fate that would await him as he followed the uncharted routes of the fulfilment of God's love; a man who will stop at nothing, not even death, is a threat full of fear and disaster to those who are not on his side.

> He finished up in the papers.
> He came to a very bad end.
> He was charged with bringing the living to life.
> No man was that prisoner's friend.

> There's only one kind of punishment
> To fit that kind of crime.
> They rigged a trial and shot him dead,
> They were only just in time.[12]

Jesus, the son born to Mary in a common stable, was executed because he dared to connect every aspect of life with the work of his Father. He was killed because he demonstrated freedom; freedom to flout constraining religious red tape, freedom to break through the conventions of status, of sex, of empty tradition, freedom to enjoy the company of the disreputable, freedom to weep with the suffering. He had to be silenced because the kind of freedom he embodied awakens undreamt of energies. By his loving and strong compassion, by his courage, men and women were liberated from the trap of mutely accepting their shackles under the conventions of the ruling parties. This is dangerous stuff to authorities whose power is maintained by quelling any disturbance in the status quo.

> In view of what he plainly said, is it any wonder that all who were rich and prosperous felt a horror of strange things, a swimming of their world at his teaching? . . . In the white blaze of this kingdom of his there was to be no property, no privilege, no pride and precedence; no motive indeed, and no reward but love. Is it any wonder that men were dazzled and blinded and cried out against him? Even his disciples cried out when he would not spare them the light. Is it any wonder that the priests realized that between this man and themselves, there was no choice, that he or their priest-craft should perish? Is it any wonder that the Roman soldiers, confronted and amazed by something soaring over their comprehension and threatening all their disciplines, should take refuge in wild laughter and crown him with thorns and robe him in purple and make a mock Caesar out of him?[13]

For if they were to take him seriously, they might, like the centurion, like Pilate's wife, feel his authority touch the very marrow of their bones. To take him seriously, to take ourselves and our neighbours seriously, is 'to enter a strange and alarming life, to abandon habits, to control instincts and impulse, to essay an incredible happiness'.[14]

We cannot protest that we are following Christ's commandment to love our neighbours as ourselves while we deliberate on how or whether to rid ourselves of intolerably evil and destructive bombs, or whether, instead, to drop them on our neighbours. Nor can we protest that we are following this commandment when we contribute 0.29 per cent of the gross national product to the Third World, which then has to return much more to us in debt repayments; nor when the rich can jump the queue for hospital treatment, leaving the poor to suffer and even die, untreated; nor when covert racial discrimination ensures that black young people are many times more likely to remain jobless and to end up with prison sentences than white young people.

Christ must have struggled with whether there could be any purpose in what appeared to be the total destruction of his life's work, as he was abandoned and handed over for public execution, yet his appalling, fierce conflict with evil continued unabated and gathered force right to his death. The difficult and uncomfortable truth is that Christ's uncompromising integrity stretched up to, and even beyond, his human limits. God's incarnate love permeates every facet of living. No part can be outside or beyond this love – not even the latest strike and my reaction to it, not even the latest cut-back on benefits to the least privileged and my response (or lack of response) to it, not even the expenditure on defence with which we prepare to kill our neighbours. National, international, domestic and deeply personal affairs are all the intimate concern of the God whose Son embodied love untainted by the effects of fear.

The kind of courage needed is that of the slight young woman on trial for her part in demonstrating at Greenham Common against nuclear defence. She, too, threatened the power of the status quo and was imprisoned for her courage in bearing witness to inconvenient truths. She stood in the dock, 'placed her two hands on her belly and said simply: "When I feel my child kicking in here, I think, 'How could I let my child come into a world threatened by nuclear weapons – and do nothing?' " '[15]

2

❧

LOSS OF HOPE

A young teacher, just setting out on her teaching career, was discussing the pros and cons of being with the five-year-olds in her reception class. Someone said to her, 'They're chaotic at that age.' She replied, 'I don't think so. I think they're very organized, but as adults we don't find it so easy to perceive their logic.' Not every teacher has the generosity to look at the young human beings in their charge like that, and there is often much misery in schools, because of the battles about conforming to examination requirements, the rigour of graded assessments, and the difficulty of fitting in with acceptable norms of socialized behaviour.

A little boy aged seven came for his very first piano lesson. J. was excited and nervous, and his nervousness spilled over into giggles. His curiosity was enormous. His hands seemed to curve naturally and easily over the keyboard. His ears were quick, and his innate intelligence and musicality grasped the principles of notation without any fuss. With the other children he was awkward and gauche; many of them considered him a sissy, because his lack of co-ordination made him handicapped for the important business of rough-and-tumble, and he was certainly no asset in competitive games. But in his piano lessons he thrived. He seemed to know about music already – it was simply a matter of reminding him of what he had always known – and here his co-ordination between hands and ears was acute and accurate. He was soon playing little pieces and needed no outward encouragement to explore, but he was also obstinate. If he did not take to an idea nothing would persuade him to give it a try; scales and arpeggios were anathema, and surreptitious routes had to be discovered to circumvent his resistance so that he could develop the technique he needed. However, there was no need to worry: the music for him was so enticing that when he was ready he would practise the exercises that would enable him to play the way he wanted to.

But after less than two years, the music teacher left the school. Another teacher arrived. She liked order and neatness. J. was not neat: biro marks scattered themselves on his clothes, his socks were always on the skew, his collar and tie never seemed to feel at ease with each other and, besides this, his organization of his musical learning was disorderly. Fingering was a nuisance, sight-reading, as a compulsory part of lessons, was a bore, and those scales and arpeggios were still to him a very unnecessary evil. The new teacher insisted on following the syllabus in a logical progression, and J.'s enthusiasm was dampened. He did not have the encouragement of parents to arm him against the listlessness that was overtaking his practising. Without the stimulus of affirmation and joy in his own discovering, he gradually found less and less reason to go to the piano. Sadly, it all tailed away, and what had been such an exciting adventure was quietly shrunk down to orthodox paths until it vanished.

This may seem only a very minor tragedy. After all music is certainly not part of the core curriculum in current educational policy. But for this little boy learning to play the piano had opened a door which revealed to him, briefly, vistas far greater than merely the sight of a cosy recreational activity. Music was in the core of his being, and it had given him a means of expressing himself, so that the other children, while still scorning his inability to kick a football or run in a straight line, had begun to respect him even at this young age for the authority with which he played the piano. Now he doubted himself and relapsed once more into a gangling, purposeless outsider.

There are, of course, countless examples of creativity growing, phoenix-like out of the burning fire of harrowing circumstances, like Beethoven's composition and Dostoevsky's novels mentioned in chapter 4. There are the self-help groups springing into life, witnessing to people's generosity in using their experience to help others. There are the many books written out of tribulation bringing immense comfort to their readers as well as healing in some sense to their authors. *As it was. And world without end* is one of these, written by Helen Thomas to try to assuage her grief after her poet-husband, Edward Thomas, was killed during the First World War. Grace Sheppard's book *An Aspect of Fear* is another, where she shares her struggle to overcome crippling fear. There are people who channel their energies in new ways after their lives appear to be totally devastated, like the widow of the diplomat assassinated in Northern Ireland, who became passionately involved in sponsoring humanitarian and community work there, enabling her to avoid the bitterness which might otherwise have eaten away and destroyed her. There are the bereaved parents who have bravely set up COPE, an organization which raises funds and offers services in the East Midlands for the children's oncology unit and other bereaved parents, after their own little daughter had died of cancer.

But it is not always like this. 'Twin disasters hit Third World', 'Over a million face starvation', 'Cyclone may have killed 100,000', 'Government denies aid fatigue' – all front-page headlines in *The Guardian* on May 3rd 1991.

How can the love of God encompass suffering on such a horrendously vast scale? The meaninglessness, the fear, the pain, the misery, the anger, the guilt, the anguish, all seem unending, and far beyond any extenuating circumstances of redeeming value. There are no ready-made answers.

'Hope deferred maketh the heart sick' (a line from Proverbs 13:12) is the title Helen Waddell gives to her retelling of the story about Joseph imprisoned in Pharoah's Egypt many centuries before Christ. I remember reading it aloud to a group of eight- and nine-year-olds and finding the hopelessness of Joseph's situation sticking like grit in my throat. One of his fellow prisoners, Pharoah's chief butler, dreamed a dream which, according to Joseph's interpretation, predicted that the butler would be summoned to return to Pharoah's court. This was exactly what happened. Joseph had hoped that the butler would remember him to Pharoah, and that he too would be released, but once freed the chief butler forgot about the young Hebrew. Joseph, who had seen another fellow captive, the chief baker, executed at Pharoah's command, languished forgotten, without hope and sick at heart for an interminable two years more. Only when all the wise men of Egypt had failed in their attempts to explain Pharoah's two strange and vivid dreams, did the chief butler expediently remember the imprisoned interpreter of dreams who might be of help to Pharoah.[1]

Most people have felt the sickening downward lurch within their bodies when a much yearned for reunion with a friend has to be cancelled, when a long-awaited job interview results in being turned down, or when a relationship is irrevocably broken. There is grey dreariness as day follows day without the possibility of the change of hue that hope once gave. The heart does feel sick; in fact the whole body can feel sick as it is drained of energy and left with only the dullness of apathy.

Deferred hope makes the heart sick. But when hope is extinguished, then meaninglessness can take its full toll. Perhaps this is why Lawrence LeShan, the American psychotherapist, works with such passionate concern with his patients who have life-threatening illnesses;[2] he asks them to dream for what they really want, he encourages them to take steps towards that dream, to be greedy for themselves and for life: in fact, to dare to hope again. The interconnectedness of body and soul means that life without hope influences the resources of the total organism; LeShan's work tries to reverse that.

Too often, working with cancer patients, one can trace a pattern where the whole body has reverberated with the sense of betrayal, and from this moment disease has set in. It may be the sickening jolt to existence when a redundancy notice is received after a long spell in a company, doing apparently well-valued work; or it may be the feeling of total rejection when one is abandoned by one's partner with whom so much has been invested.

In his book *The Informed Heart* Bruno Bettelheim writes of the prisoners who came to believe the repeated statements of the guards:

> that there was no hope for them, that they would never leave the camp except as a corpse. Such men still obeyed orders, but only blindly or automatically; no longer selectively or with inner reservation or any hatred at being so

abused. They still looked about, or at least moved their eyes around. The looking stopped much later . . . but they never did anything on their own any more. Typically this stopping of action began when they no longer lifted their legs as they walked. They only shuffled them. When finally even the looking about on their own stopped, they soon died.[3]

With loss of hope, there is no escape clause; there is no way out. It represents itself in many guises and can affect people at any stage of life. There is the indescribable despair of the infants in the Romanian orphanages, discovered after the overthrow of Ceaucescu. Not only are they underfed, unwashed and cold, they are utterly bereft. To see them is to see the most agonizing behaviour of little babies totally deprived of love. Emotionally and physically they are without hope of having their hunger satisfied.

At the other end of life, an elderly man, facing the death of his wife after a marriage of over forty years, felt that he would be facing a bleak nothingness when she went. Without her his life would be valueless. 'Without her, I'm nothing,' he wept, 'without her, I'm useless. We did everything together. Life is no use to me without her.' When she died nothing could bring back light to his life, not his children, nor even his grand-children. He hoped for death to take him. Death held no fear for him, indeed death offered the only relief, as, with the possi-bility of an afterlife, he might be united with his wife.

Diagnosis of a terminal illness can be a mortal wound to hope. And suffering is a lonely business, often messy and degrading as well. Invaded by a terminal illness, the options are narrowed startlingly; there is a contracting in what can be achieved, plan-ned, managed, even adjusted to.

A young man was struggling towards the end of his battle with Hodgkins disease. Once he had had an 80 per cent hope of cure, but now it had become plain that his immune system had insufficient resources to continue fighting much longer. He said, 'When you have 'flu you feel lousy, but you know that after a few days it will pass – you'll feel better. You will return to normal. I know now this disease isn't going to go. It puts me in a different category.' He had vomiting, painful swollen glands, diminishing eyesight, circulation difficulties, lack of energy and appetite and many other symptoms to cope with, but it was his perception of himself as separated off from his contemporaries whose lives were open-ended that was hardest to bear.

A professional woman, Miss S., was an in-patient at the hospice for maybe the fourth time since she had contracted Motor Neurone Disease. She was there for a fortnight's respite care, and she was deeply depressed. For her, it was not so much the terminal nature of the illness which was affecting her, as the consequences and limitations to her way of living.

She had been an independent, energetic person, combining a professional position with some private teaching and a creative interest in the arts. She said that for her, physical activities had stimulated her mental attitude; before her illness affected her, when things had begun to get her down in the ordinary way, she could sort herself out by some aggressive digging in the garden, or a vigorous onslaught on the painting and decorating of her home. The complementarity of physical and mental well-being worked well for her.

When she was told she would not walk again, she fought back: 'If I can't walk again, I'll buy a scooter.' She was determined to stay mobile and to search out alternatives so that she could remain numbered amongst the living, and a contributor to life as she valued it.

But the disease continued on its inexorable progress and depression began to move in. Imperceptibly, the enormity of the situation seeped into Miss S. Her mind remained clear but her muscles were decreasing in efficiency. She was being slowly prevented from engaging in every activity which had been her way of life, which had given her pleasure, joy and a sense of fulfilment. This was devastating. She had been used to taking an active part, to being a responsible worker, a community-minded citizen, a do-it-yourself enthusiast, an independent householder, the main carer for her elderly, widowed mother; the realization that she was gradually going to be stripped of all her physical assets was a sickening, mind-blowing shock.

'The first stage knocks you senseless,' she said. 'It takes a while before you can let the realization sink in.' All manner of questions which had no answers arrived and turned round and round. 'You question everything, trying to find a reason. Why me? Why this pain? What have I done to warrant this? It feels like a form of punishment: if God is a God of love, why has he picked on me? It is a terrible blow. Why have I been given this death sentence?' The questions pressed on and on, contracting her vision even more. 'You doubt everything,' she said. 'You doubt the existence of God. You doubt every belief you have ever held.'

Miss S. had previously felt contented with her role in the church. She had been much in demand as an organist; she had enjoyed the active, participatory role in the services in which this had involved her, but gradually her hands became less responsive. By this fourth visit to the hospice, her right hand was almost useless and her left hand was not so dextrous, while her shoulders were also becoming affected; she could neither play her instrument nor do the calligraphy and art work she had been able to enjoy earlier. Her inability to take refuge in activity when the going became rough chipped away at her self-esteem. She was now dependent on other people to get her washed and dressed and to put her in her chair, where she stayed all day until the nurses came to put her to bed late in the evening. The lack of privacy and dignity was deeply humiliating. She felt only a nuisance and a burden, losing confidence even in her ability to fight.

She had been delivered a death sentence. She had searched for meaning, and found none; she had questioned every aspect and found herself only more and more enmeshed in her own suffering.

'When it hits you, you are forced inwards. You consider only yourself . . . You forget the suffering of Christ.' In addition, said Miss S. 'All this sets in with depression, which is abhorrent to my own nature. So then there's guilt as well.'

Miss S., slumped in her chair, unable to heave herself into a more comfortable position, was suffused with misery; in spite of all her positive attitudes and her fighting spirit, which her doctor and others had remarked on, she was helpless against the inactivity enforced by the creeping lack of muscular response. As one of the chaplains at St Christopher's Hospice had commented to a patient with the same disease, 'It is hard to be the wounded Jew, when by nature you are the good Samaritan.'[4]

About two years before this time, I had read W. H. Vanstone's *The Stature of Waiting*.[5] It had given me cause for much thought. In it Canon Vanstone reveals again the beauty and symmetry of the human within the divine, the divine within the human, and redresses the balance which is so often askew when 'doing' is in ascendance above 'being'.

There was one key concept which hovered in the back of my mind:

> At a certain point in His life, Jesus passed from action to passion . . . from working in freedom to waiting upon what others decided and receiving what others did . . . Waiting can be the most intense and poignant of all human experiences – the experience which, above all others, strips us of affection and self-deception and reveals to us the reality of our needs, our values and ourselves . . . at the moment when Jesus is handed over in the Garden, we see Him waiting, in the agony of expectancy, for whatever it is that He is to receive.

Diffidently, I offered this to Miss S. She said she had never thought of Christ in this way, never considered him as being the still person suffering the events to unfold around him. This was something new to her. It did not resolve the difficulties, but it offered a different perspective.

A little later, in a similar vein, we talked about the brainwashing effects of our work-conscious, action-orientated society, and how difficult it was for her to allow the Mary part of her greater rein, when the Martha part had always been the more satisfying role. Her frustrations did not melt away, but a new challenge had presented itself.

Perhaps the key lies somewhere in the discussions we had about her feelings and opinions on euthanasia. To her, euthanasia was the solution she felt she needed when life was no longer worth living, and she considered that euthanasia should be made a viable option by overcoming the present legal prohibitions.

On bad days, the frustration of being rendered increasingly incapable, while becoming through the illness ever more reliant on others, made her suspect that bureaucracy and incompetence were blocking her way and preventing her from making the best use of what time she had left. With the feeling that time was running out and that total paralysis was creeping upwards, she was driven to the conclusion that not only did no one care, and that no one was making the necessary efforts on her behalf, but that she herself was of no value. She felt herself to be a worthless drain on resources – financial, nursing and emotional – thus, euthanasia offered a powerful alternative to this painful wrestling with a slow, living dying. But on good days, when she felt cared for, treated as a human being, when her dignity was respected and she was not 'handled like a sack of coal', then euthanasia as a choice was far away. Of course she suffered mood swings from this illness, and it was not only her inner attitudes that altered, it was her perception of the attitudes of the people around her that made a great deal of difference to her feelings of worth and her hope.

She and I had been intrigued with how interested she had been in discussing ideas for this book, and how this had been stimulating in itself. Nothing in her situation changed to the outside eye, but thinking about a chapter on 'Loss of Hope' seemed to counteract meaninglessness for her.

Some months after her collaboration on this chapter, she was fitted with a 'Possum' (an electronic device) which enabled her to use the telephone, open the front door and enjoy a small degree of independence. A week before her death, her doctor came to visit her and noticed in her a peace and serenity that she had not seen before. A few days later Miss S. phoned the doctor using the Possum. This was her final act; she became unconscious within minutes of the phone call and died within a couple of hours. It seems that her grappling with the different aspects of Martha and Mary continued right to the end, but the tranquillity which her doctor observed during the last week was some kind of recognition of the positive value of the stature of waiting. It was something which had eluded her for most of her illness, but right at the end she discovered a way of managing the balance so that she died both in control and at peace.

The young man I wrote of earlier who had fought so valiantly against Hodgkins disease and felt himself in some way marginalized by terminal illness – isolated from the rest of us who have normal life expectations – found some kind of comfort in seeing his life within the much greater arena of the survival of the planet. He had gone through trial by chemotherapy with its accompanying nauseating side-effects, often causing him worse dread than the disease itself. Radiotherapy had been tried too. For him there was now no hope of reprieve, and he was frightened by his lack of control over the increasing pain and heavy weariness which invaded him; yet he was still sometimes able to see the humorous side of things and still wanting to put what energy he had into ecological issues. He supported green issues: he saw humankind as the main enemy of this earth, an enemy easily capable of destroying this beautiful world which he revelled in. He wanted to do what he could to ensure this did not happen. He urged those who would to put money into saving the Amazonian rain forests.

During the days when he felt slightly better, he loved walking with a companion or two in the fields or in the woods, or seeing the countryside from a car. He enjoyed planning and planting his new garden, even though he knew he would not be around to savour the full fruition of his plans; many friends and relations offered manpower, or plants, and came round to admire the garden's progress. His courage lasted right to the end in spite of his fear and pain and the welling of his tears of regret at having to bid farewell to everything he had ever known.

Nothing can make the clocks go back; there is no way of doing a re-run to alter the circumstances which have apparently obliterated all hope. The situation remains stark; but sometimes an inner shift of attitude can bring comfort to a barren place.

Some words of John Fenton's seem to sum up with great clarity this part of the journey:

> What we fear most is our weakness and incompetence, whereas what we should fear is our blindness. Our

inabilities are our strengths, because they are the essential precondition for service of Christ and the action of God. Nothing is more destructive than the assurance that one can hope on one's own.[6]

We need hope, and we need our fellow pilgrims to hope with us.

POSTSCRIPT: Fragments of hope

I am awed by the anguish and the honesty of the love with which a friend accepts her son as he is imprisoned for a serious criminal offence.

I am humbled by the courage and tenacity of a young man I have just met; his body is slowly succumbing, over a decade, to the devastation of a terminal illness.

A man approaches me with such delighted recognition and tenderness I am almost crying. Where does he find such reservoirs of love when he is suffering the anguish of knowing his son died in mental torment?

I read the prayer found on a scrap of paper after their death written by some women from Ravensbrück concentration camp; they plead with God to deal mercifully with their torturers, to forget the agonies they perpetrated on them, and to remember only the qualities of the fruits of love such atrocities inspired.[7] I am overwhelmed by such Christ-like generosity. This kind of loving is of a different order; it is breathtaking.

I read of Etty, a young Dutch Jewess who wrote in her diaries during the gradually accumulating horror of the Nazi persecution of her race. As the darkness of the holocaust descended and shrouded her life, 'she poured out her heart to God: "One thing is becoming increasingly clear to me: that you cannot help us: that we must help you to help ourselves." ' There could be no physical rescue, no material rescue from the inexorable grinding on of the unspeakable pain of the present. 'That is all we can manage these days and also all that matters: that we safeguard that little piece of you, God, in ourselves.'[8]

The power of that mystical understanding of the immanent and transcendent presence of God is almost beyond my recognition.

Could divine love be in me? Like that?

For me, the line in the collect, 'the good things which pass man's understanding' and the final clause, 'that we, loving you above all things, may obtain your promises which exceed all that we can desire'[9] have always been to do with yearning for fuller, more loving relationships. Now, however, within the glimpses of this different quality of loving which can transcend our earthed humanness, it all seems to mean far more than that: God's promises are concerned with transforming and redeeming, and can penetrate even the dark, intolerable, derelict places in life.

I have no desire to learn through pain. Yet I also know that I want to live my life to the full. I want to experience, in Stephen Verney's words, that 'the best wine is just exactly now'[10] which means discovering the possibilities in every moment, not confining my perception of God's presence to the joyful moments only.

Can I really let that kind of learning percolate through to me?

Could I now dare to let 'Jesus on the cross point me down into those depths of horror where human beings torture one another in prison camps – into that abyss of anguish where we experience what it is to be abandoned and where we come to know that human life itself doesn't make sense – and then point me deeper still', to the hope beyond despair, 'where shining out of the horror is the glory of love, so that we can receive out of that anguish the transforming power of love'?[11]

Have I really the courage to trust this truth as I now see it, being persuaded that nothing can separate us from the love of God, neither death, however it approaches, nor life, in whatever guise it arrives: neither things present, in this minute but supremely important movement of living, nor things to come, in the unknown, unforeseeable future?[12]

Can I face the paradox now revealed to me? On the one hand I need to let go, child-like, into the ever-present guidance of the compassionate embrace of God's love; on the other hand, I must take up full adult responsibility towards the stark choices with which this love will surely confront me.

The magnitude of it appalls me. But I have to begin, for faith means more even than trusting in this truth: it involves me in beginning 'to act in accordance with it'.[13] So I begin, one step at a time, knowing that I cannot do even that on my own: I need, in my humanness, the encouragement of the Divine Presence in the form of my fellow human beings. And I need to carry with me the conviction of Harry Williams, that 'we haven't begun to be disciples of Jesus until we know something, a very little of the joy – with which He endured the cross',[14] and a glimmer of confidence in the very great love with which our Lord is willing to accompany each one of us.

3

THE ANGUISH OF THE MIND

I, a stranger and afraid,
in a world I never made.

Thou tellest my flittings; put my tears into thy bottle;
are not these things noted in thy book? (*Psalm 56:8*)

The day before Frank died, he rang us up. He had had a terrible night, he said, half waking, half sleeping with a tremendous pain in his chest. 'What are you doing now?' I asked; and he said 'Waiting for the ambulance. I just wanted to tell you I love you very much. I must go now, goodbye.' From 120 miles away, I called some of his other friends to make sure he was visited in the Norwich Infirmary. So it was that his closest friend, Jack, a Methodist Minister and bus driver, was with him shortly before he died peacefully.

Frank was a suffering servant. He seemed to have a vocation to suffer. He was one of those human beings who seemed compelled to take on more suffering than is just. His personal pilgrimage took him into many strange byways. He studied Scientology for ten years and underwent the 'clearing' procedures demanded by that discipline, together with the emotional disturbance and trauma which seem to accompany it. He subjected himself for weeks at a time to the arduous spiritual and physical routine of Coombe Springs, a centre which followed the teaching of Gurdjieff and numbered the actress Eva Bartok among its followers. He studied Ouspensky, and admired and

43

studied with J. G. Bennett. All the time he never failed to hold fast to the Christian way, and to attend mass (as he always put it) regularly.

Frank and I met as he was a member of the small weekday congregation of the church which I served. This complex, many-sided man became very important to me. I even found him in my dreams – once as an architect supervising a building site! Most of all, he reminded me that I was a priest, especially when I really wanted to forget it. He was old enough to be my father, but often called me 'Father', usually when I said something theologically fatuous. 'Father,' he once said, 'what is the meaning of the wedding garment?' (see Matthew 22:11, 12). The question fascinated him. Maybe it meant to him the clothing of a fully developed soul. Because it fascinated him, his friends were often compelled to question their commitment to Christ and to his church. He expected godliness and commitment from his priest-friends, and would take them down a peg or two gently but pointedly, smoking his pipe the while.

In many ways Frank embodied in his own self the theme of the anguish of the mind. Born in 1917, his childhood was not a particularly happy one. His mother was devoted to him and he to her, but references to father were missing and it seems that this was out of charity to a man who drank too much and was occasionally violent. He spoke often, however, of teenage influences which set him upon a literary career: a headmaster and his wife who befriended him and introduced him to poetry and the coterie of young men who were involved with the Maddermarket theatre under the direction of Nugent Monck. Father Pitts of St James, Pockthorpe, a radical pre-Second World War Anglo-Catholic priest and social reformer, guided him in his growing faith and encouraged him to serve at the altar at early morning weekday masses.

Frank thus developed an independent mind, thinking through the imperatives of Christian faith and discovering the way of his own personal pilgrimage, a way which led him first to pacifism, then to become a leading member of the Peace Pledge Union and then to being a conscientious objector during the war (we shall see where this led him, later in the chapter). It did, however, further increase his sense of being an outsider. Early on, before the onset of puberty, he had become aware that he found other boys attractive, and adolescence increased his awareness that the female sex evoked in him no particular attraction, although later he was to enjoy several long and deep platonic friendships with women.

Does the homosexual person always have to suffer? Perhaps it is not inevitable in today's ethical climate, but there is no doubt that Frank suffered.

Frank wrote long letters to me about his perceptions of life. These letters were written by a man who had wrestled with the problem of feeling he did not fit in with society for most of his seventy-odd years. He felt, as he said in his seventieth birthday party speech, like the actor who walks on to the stage and finds he is in a different play and does not know his part. I have included passages from his long letter to me of May 1986, as it is better for him to tell the tale in his own unique, self-mocking, humorous tone.

In the midst of a letter about the strangeness of human character, he wonders about the difference between him and his heterosexual brother:

Maybe it has a lot to do with being queer!

I, a stranger, and afraid
In a world I never made.

Well what, inter alia, I am trying to say is that my homosexuality is as central to me as your love for Sarah (and the children) is to you. It is a built-in bias, not just a prejudice!

I first, with hindsight, had my earliest homoerotic fantasy when being pushed in a pram. I must have been 2 or perhaps 3! Although I was nearly out of my teens before I had full-blown homoerotic experiences, my early and mid teens were dominated by intense devotions successively to 2 or 3 other boys, although quite 'Platonic'; I mean just confining physical expression to rather solemn and ceremonious hand shaking or a very occasional chance hug in wrestling or horseplay – actually nothing that even the most severe moralist could call sin (except for a Methodist schoolmaster who seemed to scent Gomorrah if he saw two boys laughing and walking together: well, you can't be too careful can you?). [See chapter 5 for the story of Jim, whose life was blighted by this suspicion.]

But I was an omnivorous reader and by 13 was dipping into religion (Newman's *Apologia Pro Vita Sua*) and psychology. I came upon an Outline of abnormal psychology by Charles Baudouin (if my memory serves me right!) and there I found to my infinite horror and dismay that my intense devotions, successively to B., J. and A. were evidence of a deep and despicable perversion, along with necrophilia, sadism, coprophilia, and God knows what, examples of which were detailed and enumerated in an Appendix of case histories. Was I then indeed reading my own biography? I was a very troubled little boy! Certainly there was no one I could even think of talking to about it.

In this way, Frank ate of the tree of knowledge and knew good and evil. At the same time, he was cast out of the Garden of Eden and his return was blocked by an angel with a flaming sword. No matter that these existed in his own mind: here was the beginning of an imposed guilt with which he struggled all his life, in common with many who find difficulty with their sexuality. This must be guilt by association; for no reasoned and objective moral position will consider homoerotic feelings and devotion to be a perversion. It is rather the assumptions of thoughtless and care-less people which create the hatred and fear in society, and which turn the Garden of Love into a place of fear and uncertainty.

And Priests in black gowns were walking their rounds,
And binding with briars my joys and desires.[1]

Who can tell what tortures of a similar nature attended the life and death of the scoutmaster who is mentioned in Frank's next sentence in the same letter:

I did remember that recently, a very nice scoutmaster, who

46

helped to take us when I was a Scout, suddenly committed suicide, and he was only mentioned by adults in very hushed and shocked whispers. About this time, I had in the first place, (because my adored B., 4 years my senior, was an altar server there), begun to attend every service on Sundays and early services during the week, at St Leonard's Church.[2]

So, by 14, I had become an earnest little pacifist, just to complicate life a bit more, and a year later was running a Sunday School and thinking about socialism.

It is a normal part of growing up to suffer intellectual pain, as one discovers the real-life effects of existing and unexpected ideas. But the additional agony of awakening to the perceived status of the gay person, especially in the thirties, should be better known than it is. The next part of Frank's letter gives an insight: he gained employment at the library under Fred Henderson, 'for several decades Chairman of the Libraries Committee and for even longer a Marxist theoretician of international fame'.

A certain young female library assistant (S.) had the duty each morning of going to the Staffroom and making mid-morning tea or coffee. I followed her up and indulged in quite mild kissing – certainly no deep petting! My advances were not resisted but one dreadful morning, her fiancé, a staff member several years my senior, came in and caught us. S., who had a normal endowment of survival instinct, more or less yelled 'RAPE', and I was taken before the head librarian. A solemn inquest followed. Every female on the staff was separately interviewed to see if they had cause to complain of my conduct. I was threatened with suspension! Actually I was rather pleased since I was doing my best to establish a heterosexual image. God should at least give me one mark for trying, but I do not suppose He will, since we are told He is a hard man, gathering where He has not sown etc.

Frank's experience underlines a pattern which he did not seem to have realized, at that stage of his development, was only too common: an intertwining between sex and religion in human development. It was Jung who succinctly commented that if a client came to him with a spiritual problem, there was invariably a sexual problem and vice versa. But then, for Frank, the pleasant and unpleasant guilt of this awareness within him of the interconnectedness of sexuality and spirituality became compounded with the evil of fundamentalism. We go back to him at the age of thirteen:

> . . . being a pious little boy and eager to learn of God's plan for mankind, I began to read one chapter each day from a large family Bible. This was copiously annotated by some 19th century protestant divine, named . . . Browne, I think. Naturally I began with Genesis, Chapter One, reading carefully, not only the sacred text, but Mr Browne's annotations. Then one fateful morning I got to the sin of Onan[3] and the notes made it abundantly clear that I had in my ignorance (although, indeed, I must confess, with considerable pleasure!) been committing the dreadful sin of self-pollution! At the same time I had noticed to my puzzlement (since I had never seen an older boy or man naked), a growth of hair around my penis! I decided this must be a mark of Cain, an evidence of my sin. (Mr. – or I am sure *Doctor* – Browne's hints of dreadful penalties were terrifying, but not explicit). And I carefully shaved the dreadful hair off with much prayer to God for forgiveness!

Frank's next, ironic comment on this phase of his life is both hopeful and sad; for me too it is sad, as to my knowledge the churches still do not come to grips or even handshakes with the complexities of the joys and delights and the potential for pain in sexuality at any stage, let alone at confirmation.

> In my confirmation class the only reference to sex was that it was something sacred that happened in marriage. I dare say that nowadays very full instruction is given, maybe with diagrams and working models [sic!]. But I very much hope (though my hope is slender) that the class will not be told that sex is only about a boy (or girl) meeting a girl

(or boy) and getting married in holy heterosexual wedlock, for, if that is the teaching, some very frightened little boy (or girl) may well end up hating the Church and hating God!

It will be recalled that this letter is from a 70-year-old man who has, through his spiritual pilgrimage, largely come to terms with and accepted his homosexuality. But only a few years previously, with full media coverage, the local bishop had once again asserted the traditional 'Christian' condemnation of homosexuality, and again Frank was evidently deeply hurt, as were many of his friends. I remember feeling very indignant and trapped by the institution: alas, I did not speak out at the time.

Originally, as a young man, Frank had entered psychotherapy and studied philosophy. He produced a picture of his life which he expressed as follows:

> So! My then contemporary friendship with L.: could it really be reduced in meaning and value to my reactions to father? [The Freudian influence.] All I loved at that time and all we did and thought about together, music, poetry, walking in the countryside, indeed all my thoughts and feelings were intermeshed with my feelings for L. I did not like to think this, but was prepared to go along with it, paint my pictures, make my clay models, record my dreams and indeed interpret all my present in terms of the past. The assumption was of course that events truly significant in this past, the nasty things seen in the wood-shed, could, with work and patience, be recalled, re-lived, their effect discharged and then, going back to 'square one', the place where the river of life took the wrong turn, one re-lived the lost childhood, grew into the normal hetero-sexual nature intended – justified, as you theologians might say, though not finally sanctified of course until one had succeeded in a job, married and had the right number of children etc.

I do not know when these hopes faded. But fortunately they did, and Frank seems to have accepted his gayness as a natural part of his psyche, which in turn was directed outwards as a loving warmth of character. Though to some he remained an angular man, difficult to approach and hidden behind thick glasses and impassive expression, most of his friends found Frank becoming the deeply accepting, risk-taking, hospitable person Alan Webster, former Dean of Norwich Cathedral, described in his funeral tribute:

> He never rejected young or old, reasonable or unreasonable, no-one but the angels will ever know how often he gave a bed or a meal at his home. In conversation too, he did not reject ideas which convention found embarrassing or even dangerous. There was something about Frank like another great Anglican layman, Samuel Johnson, always prepared to think, to bounce ideas around.[4]

Despite occasional attacks of 'the horrors', which may have been more to do with his relationship with his father than his gay nature, Frank accepted his place in a largely homophobic society cheerfully, but the cost was enormous. This is borne out by his comment about weddings: 'Considering that at weddings, I feel somewhat like an Orthodox Jew being compelled to act as an acolyte at a High Mass, though I says it as shouldn't, I think I behave rather well at weddings.' In the same letter, he goes on to describe how he had been told that he had been the life and soul of the party at the marriage of one of the handsome young men with whom he had fallen in love.

Can we now acknowledge what a virtue true homosexual love can be? Recently, the Church of England has demonstrated the beginnings of such understanding,[5] and promised much. But it remains to be seen if the pattern of hatred and prejudice of many sections of the churches is to be transformed. The medieval mystical writer Aelred of Rievaulx wrote a complete treatise on the importance of friendship, entitled *De Spirituali Amica*.[6] Gordon Wakefield writes of the work, 'There is much here that our sex-obsessed age, which has gone far to make friendship impossible, needs to relearn.' I, too, am conscious of undervaluing friendship and am ashamed to catch myself occasionally regarding with amused suspicion the love between friends of the same sex: I am, unavoidably, tainted by the values of our age, which tends to see a gay friendship wherever men express affection for one another. It is a deeply ingrained and false attitude in many heterosexual people that it matters whether or not this is so. The values of our age in relation to gayness are nevertheless more open than in Frank's pre-war days. There are perhaps some advantages in our more tolerant society, and maybe fewer gay friends are persecuted, except, possibly, if they are clergymen.

Alan Webster told us at his funeral that Frank had dreamed Walt Whitman's dream 'of the city invincible to the attacks of the rest of the earth, I dreamed that was the new city of friends.' Frank 'valued his friends as old-time navigators valued the stars to find their way in a dark world. In his favourite words, "We took sweet counsel together and walked in the house of God as friends." '

Frank interpreted his hospitality as coming from an imperative he had fully accepted.

> Those I have sheltered I have taken in because I have been told to, over 45 years, by psychoanalyst, doctor, psychiatrist, girl friends (!) of theirs, and of course dear priests! Sometimes, quite literally I have found people at my cottage etc., I have never heard of before. They have been on my doorstep. They have been in various degrees – junkie, psychopathic, criminal, schizophrenic, drug-addicted or perhaps just temporarily on their beam ends. Now I have defended myself to myself, and sometimes to others, by saying I have never gone out to seek waifs and strays, but if they turn up on my doorstep, what am I to do?

Did Frank keep open house for the hurt because that was the only way he thought he could earn acceptance? Did he feel that if he closed his doors to the rejected, he would have felt exposed to rejection because he was refusing others? I do not know; but in Alan Webster's words, 'all his days, he felt energetic empathy for the drop outs, the oppressed and those rejected by society or by the church'. His example was among the spurs to my own positive responses to the Night Shelter people. But his spiritual and emotional development, his 'wrestling', seems to have equipped him to cope with a variety of strange and difficult people. The difficulty of coping should not be underestimated, as Frank himself admitted of his experiences:

> They have sometimes been the occasions of great expenditure in money, time, heartbreak and sometimes public social disgrace . . . Perhaps in some instances they have survived (and even in one or two cases made good) when they might not always − there was Stephen, on heroin, who ended his life, just when I thought he was OK. He was brought to me 'for a few days', at midnight one day by Dr. Q. and another man [from a psychiatric hospital in Norwich.] Of course no-one told me he was on the hard stuff.

I mentioned at the beginning of this chapter that we should return to Frank's involvement in the war as a conscientious objector. It cannot have been common for prisoners-of-war to be befriended after the war was over, but Frank met Karl Renner in April 1946. He was from South Baden, then aged twenty-two and came from farming parents. He had one brother and five sisters and was Roman Catholic. In a letter, Frank wrote, 'In the spring and summer of 1946 he came to my flat several evenings a week and I took him out every Sunday. Then he moved to various camps at Ely and then Friday Bridge and I could only see him on Sundays or on my day off and then only briefly.' With his friend Sybil ('the nearest thing I ever had to a sister'), Frank entertained Karl during his days in Norwich. He had realized how much Karl missed his sisters, so Sybil and Karl would sing German folksongs while Frank prepared supper. Karl returned home in the spring of 1947.

Then Frank's adventurous spirit took over.

> I tried unsuccessfully to enter Germany in the summer of 1948 to see him − quite illegally, since no civilians were permitted to visit Germany − and finally got arrested by Swiss Police. In 1949, although the French military zone (in which Baden was situated) was still closed to visitors,

I did manage to get through by using lots of local railway journeys.

. There in South Baden, on the farm with Karl's family, a sad tale of suffering emerged which was to remain significant for the whole of Frank's life. The Renner family were warmly hospitable to Frank. He was shown round the farm in the glorious sunshine. The girls made a fuss of him and he enjoyed himself with his few words of German. A few days after his arrival he was walking in the fields with one of the girls. They passed a mound in the corner of a field. The girl crossed herself. Later Frank pieced together the story, which moved him deeply, perhaps because it was about a lonely anguished man, whose normal young desires were totally forbidden by the circumstances in which he found himself, causing him intolerable suffering.

During the war, a Polish prisoner was allocated to the Renners' farm as an extra worker. It was not much better than slave labour. He worked for his keep and shelter. We can imagine the suffering of this simple and lonely Pole, separated from his family by hundreds of miles, compelled to work on a farm where he was forbidden to fraternize with the family, and in any case, not understanding much that was said. He was given accommodation in the hayloft of the cattle byre. He was well enough fed. Karl's sisters also worked on the farm and the Pole was constantly aware of their vivacious femininity. If they had provoked the Pole in the same way as they had flashed their eyes at Frank, so much the worse. In spring, all the world of nature came alive and the Pole's young body responded too. The girls were so near, yet so far: untouchable.

One warm spring night, one of the girls wandered out into the courtyard and heard a noise in the cattle byre. She walked over and dimly saw a figure at the back of the byre. It was the Pole, driven by sexual desire, seeking his relief. The girl was appalled and ran to tell her older sister. As she ran she betrayed her presence to the Pole, who turned and saw that his shame was discovered.

The next day, the farm went about its business. The Pole

was absent. One of the farm workers found him in the cattle byre, hanging from one of the beams.

It was a Catholic district. The rule for suicides was clear: they may not be buried in consecrated ground. Thus the Pole was buried in the corner of a field on the farm.

No wonder that this story remained alive for Frank. He felt as alone as the Pole. At one time he sent me a series of his dreams, including one which he entitled 'The Backward Child', which reveals his loneliness. In this dream he is in church with a young man whom he takes home. It becomes apparent that the young man was retarded in some way. In the dream the young man becomes a child and shows his delight in a neighbour's chat. At the end of the dream he is lying on Frank's cottage doorstep as a child of six or seven. Commenting on the dream, he says, 'I have never, even in fantasy, been able to imagine myself loved and accepted, except by someone mentally defective, in special need, and feeling condemned, like me, to be a "loner".'

In his greatest suffering, when the anguish of his mind was reinforced externally by the shingles which spread to his eye during 1984, Frank again referred to the Pole. His pain was like a bee stinging in his eye every few minutes, and because he could not see to read, his dearest consolation was denied him. He could only just see to write, and his usually illegible writing became impossible. He had tried the conventional Christian response I learned at theological college, if not before:

> I have tried to offer it up. On behalf of the Pole actually . . . I never actually met him, just found his very lonely and isolated grave and wondered about him. It is not a nice story. So now if ever I have a bit of spare pain, I try to say, grinding my teeth, 'Here, Christ, you had better have this for the Pole'.

This was one of the ways Frank coped with his suffering. The figure on the cross continued to compel his attention, as it always had. A holiday in Malta, where he saw the lurid crucifixes in the churches and relished the deep piety of the ordinary people, was a great solace to him when his shingles was at its worst. He sought relief at a clinic in Norwich where he was given an electronic device which reduced the pain. He also tried Shiatzu as a complementary therapy,[7] with some degree of success. But it was the spiritual dimension which provided him with the means of coming through: the conundrums of faith in this world of technical prowess and intellectual rationalization: the profound importance for our age of the Revelations of Divine Love shown to Julian of Norwich in the fourteenth century:[8] the place of mysticism in the midst of both squalor and progress. These were all rich sources for Frank to explore with his ever seeking soul. He suffered pain on many levels and sought relief through many byways which gave him a breadth and a generosity of spirit and an honesty it was sometimes awe-inspiring to experience. Was it because of the pain that he dared to take so many risks, that he became a resource both conventional and unconventional for so many others?

POSTSCRIPT: Six Haiku for Mary
by Frank Sayer

1 THE IMMACULATE CONCEPTION

> Fair intended soil
> Prepared for the Gardener
> Who shall sow himself.

2 THE ANNUNCIATION

> He, always waiting,
> Saw Your door was left unlatched.
> Smiling, he went in.

3 CHRISTMAS

> Wandering Maiden
> You, pregnant through sunless days,
> Give birth to the Lamb.

4 THE CIRCUMCISION OF OUR LORD

Unblemished Adam
Named all creatures but You name
Their wounded Maker.

5 EASTER

Your tears thawed the earth
And the Syrian garden
Blossoms with Your Son.

6 THE GLORIOUS ASSUMPTION

Woman, crowned with stars,
Today we shall adorn You
With wheat and roses.

4

OUT OF TOUCH

I think it was Sartre who coined the phrase 'Hell is other people'. But there is a profound sense in which the opposite can also be true, and hell is an existence where other people cannot be reached, a place without other people.

I do not mean by this that being alone is hellish. Solitude in itself often has creative or restorative properties. Many people choose to live alone because they need solitariness. They need more aloneness than is generally allowed in the incessant and harsh interchange of busy-ness induced by the modern pace of living. Some people choose to be alone during periods of varying length, for the change in perspective such solitude gives, for the chance of recouping their energies, recharging their batteries. This out-of-touchness is through choice: for some it may be heaven-sent aloneness and very far from being hell.

Anthony Storr's book, *Solitude*,[1] explores this in a fascinating way, giving insight into the advantages and gains from being alone, as well as describing the painful circumstances which may have given rise to the aloneness. He writes from the viewpoint, that

> modern psychotherapists, including myself have taken as their criterion of emotional maturity the capacity of the individual to make mature relationships on equal terms. With few exceptions, psychotherapists have omitted to consider the fact that the capacity to be alone is also an aspect of emotional maturity.

At the end of his introduction, he writes:

57

Perhaps the need of the creative person for solitude, and his preoccupation with internal processes of integration can reveal something about the needs of the less gifted, more ordinary human being, which is at the time of writing [1988] neglected.

Much of the greatest work the world has ever known has arisen from solitude of one kind or another. As Anthony Storr's book demonstrates, even enforced solitude, occasioned by circumstances as varied as the arrest and imprisonment which Dostoyevsky suffered, or the profound deafness which excluded Beethoven from the normal world of sound and hearing, can be fertile ground which nurtures genius.

But enforced solitude is not always experienced as creative. Human beings are generally social beings – gregarious in one way or another – and controlling powers have used solitary confinement as a punishment, or inflicted it as a torture, throughout the ages. Enforced solitude is a most terrible deprivation, and is often unmitigated hell. Jackie Mann described it as a living hell; he had been held for 865 days as a hostage in the Middle East, and during the whole of that time of captivity he had never seen another human face. Brian Keenan, who was released from being held hostage in August 1990, said 'The constant blindfolds, the prolonged days in the dark, sometimes weeks without light create times of insanity which drive men deep, deep into themselves.'[2]

The utter loneliness of being out of touch with humankind is living in this kind of hell – where hell is without other people – a hell where you want to reach out to your fellow human beings but are unable to do so.

An extreme form of this being out of touch is the loneliness of insanity; it is the appalling loneliness of being beyond the reach of all normal human contact, where life is perpetually a tortured existence, where reality is obscured and even obliterated, and communication is for ever distorted.

The hell of mental illness impressed itself on me with renewed force recently as I sat miserably impotent beside a newly bereaved widow while she deteriorated in terror, until, consumed by fear, she was rolling around on the floor, banging and bruising herself. There was not one second of her waking day now when she could feel even the most infinitely tiny flutter of ordinary peace. She was in torment, until a sleeping pill at 10.00 p.m. shut out the pain and suffering for a few short hours. Earlier, she had whispered in a panic-stricken voice that she was terrified of being on her own, which was how she experienced her new circumstances of living in the marital home without her husband. Now her fear was driving her into even more intense aloneness. Her behaviour was communicating her terror. It seemed, however, that she was trying to communicate something more than that as well, but she was using a language which no one else could understand. She could not translate and none of us could interpret. She was utterly alone.[3] There was no way anyone could reach her, and no one knew what was going on inside her torment.

A friend of mine, who for years suffered the mental hell of schizophrenia, when she was frighteningly out of touch with safety and normality, wrote recently of the pain she experienced at that time. The pain began when she was very young and the security she needed was not there for her. As a young adult, at the time of the birth of her own first child, the pain exploded into mental illness as her baby was taken away for adoption. People with good intentions acted upon what they considered to be the right decisions, but it seemed to her that her aching love for her child was not part of that decision-making. The passage she has written gives a glimpse of the hell she found herself in during the years of her illness, when the normal boundaries of sanity could not withstand the strain.

> What is reality? Is it all an illusion? Do we not all perceive the unreality of our own periscopic view of reality? We would all be surprised if the views of our nearest and dearest were ever fully divulged. Robbie Burns was sage with his lines,
>
> > O wad some Pow'r the giftie gie us
> > To see oursels as others see us!
> > It wad frae mony a blunder free us,
> >   And foolish notion.[4]

So, the illusion is a mantle of disguise which we don on waking up.

I am not the Virgin Mary with my love-child, conceived in pathetic ignorance in a shrine on top of an Italian mountain. But I feel privileged to know how She must have felt.

Yes, he is special. He is the Son of God (or was he conceived of God?).

One's view of God in people can be all an illusion.

The finger is pointed of shame.

I wonder if She had to walk this path – another reason for fleeing to Egypt? The story does not enlarge. What were the mores and values then?

Has it always been so? Put on sackcloth and ashes.

Who has blighted whose life? Beauty had a thorn: the rose was sweet, but when I touched the stem my skin was torn.

The pain was no illusion, the pain of the loss of a first-born. Oh! Those wailing women. But there was no body to grieve over, only a parting, the cutting of the cord of life – the bond of breast to lip. That parting fragmented the mind.

Their need is greater than mine. But the arms are cut off.

The deadness of all feeling. The utter loss, even now, is too much.

Should have died. Did, in an odd sort of way. Went on living, in a vacuum, on an island of misery – functioning in a remote way. It did not hurt any more. There was NO feeling – a piece of wood floating like jetsam in a land of strangeness amongst strange people, who thought different thoughts, whose culture was of a different kind.

Is this out of context?

This passage reveals the peculiar and frightening feeling of being out of touch with other people; they appear to be foreigners, to be distant, and utterly without understanding of her perception of reality. She goes on to describe the defences she needed to employ to protect her vulnerability, and to create some kind of sense of what she had been enduring.

On go the blinkers. It is too real; it is stark, staring, blind-ingly real. No. Put the covers on, get life out of this context. Run away. Where to? Where is a safe place?

What is a safe place?

Family betrayal – no plane of understanding to stand on. Close to the earth, there is security. Does it matter how you found it? The rest is unnecessary for a while.

Then the cover must be put on again. The mantle of consciousness must cover the inequalities and barbs of meaning – the un-meaning thrusts of envy, hatred. Who else can adequately ease their own conscience, if they do not wrap others in sackcloth and ashes?

This woman still feels sharp pangs of remembered pain when her granddaughter asks her for a hug. How could it be other-wise when a cuddle was the very thing her own mother was unable to give her? The pain is only just below the surface even now and she is still to some extent aware of it although she has successfully held down a steady job for twelve or more years and has more recently ventured into wider spheres working for the local community in her spare time – a wounded pilgrim who has found a new and constructive way of continuing her journey.

Among the mentally ill are those who have been accused, or who accuse themselves, of somehow deliberately courting disaster although there seems no element of choice. They hear harsh voices saying 'You've brought this upon yourself', and some fear that the accusations are true: that in some unwitting way, they have invited this very painful condition to take over, yet they felt only the compulsion of the driving forces propel-ling them into confusion – into neurosis, into demonic fears, into depression or into psychosis. Such accusations only inten-sify the suffering. There may or may not be truth in the remark that I once heard in a television documentary that it takes courage to cross the line and let go into mental illness. But to the sufferer, courage is the last thing he or she may be aware of: most sufferers would do anything to be free of the illness, so that life without pain can be resumed.

Often when I am with someone who is mentally ill I find I

am pervaded by a strange sense of awe, and at the same time I feel a terrible sadness, a yearning to understand, and a helpless, dragging, frustrating impotence. I think the sense of awe is to do with the amazing complexity of the human brain. The brain is the storehold of memory; it has incredible powers of learning, deciphering, computing, understanding, coding and decoding, and responding, which continue night and day inside the skull of each man, woman and child. All this is taken for granted millions of times a day in our ordinary transactions, but somehow it becomes more explicitly complicated when something goes awry. It becomes apparent that what we are aware of is only the minutest tip of a vast iceberg. With someone who is suffering from mental disturbance, it can seem as if we are trying to communicate like two radio hams who find all the wavelengths are jammed. A word or a sentence may get through, but the context is wrong and the sense isn't clear, because it is distorted by the interference which is continually disrupting the efficiency of the receiving instruments.

The anguished frustration which this causes is naturally experienced most acutely by those who are closest emotionally. As a mentally ill person becomes increasingly inaccessible, the partner (or the parents or the children) can feel that all their attempts to get through to the other are floundering against impenetrable and intractable barriers. There is for them desperate, piercing distress. 'Where have we gone wrong?' 'What could I have done differently?' 'What can I do?' Questions like these pursue them continuously as they meet with behaviour that seems utterly incomprehensible, unreasonable, illogical, irrational, groundless. Each one of these people is in the keenly distressing hell of being unable to reach the person they thought they knew and loved: the out-of-touchness is there on both sides.

The anger and distress experienced by the parents of a young lad who was repudiating all approaches, rejecting all possible lines of help, in what seemed to be an arbitrary pattern of unremittingly bitter and destructive behaviour, were excruciatingly painful. Their relationship with him was in danger of becoming scarred to the point of no repair. It did seem that the son could manage somewhat better when removed from the family home – for the mother particularly, an exceedingly painful solution. It meant some relief from the intolerable and apparently evil and malevolent assaults upon family life that living in close proximity evoked, but it was a high price to pay.

Both parents had wanted their son to grow towards independence and maturity, and they had tried to foster this by their attitude towards him. They had encouraged him, as far as their ordinary means would allow, in his own interests and hobbies, and supported him both practically and emotionally. His siblings had thrived in this nurturing environment and were fully involved in adventuring outwards and finding their own self-control and self-determination. But now with him it seemed that total impasse had been reached. His mother, apparently discarded on one level and yet seemingly needed on another, felt like a caretaker; she found herself feeling an angry, helpless, grim despondency about the outcome. Professionals seemed as much on the outside and as powerless to get to grips with the difficulties as she was. She was very afraid his life was now endangered, that the destructive behaviour which no one could understand would turn inwards and in his despair her son would become suicidal.

With a friend one day, she went to light a candle for her son in the local church. She could not at present get near him in any sense, but there was a little ease for the aching heaviness inside her in this symbolic gesture, and there was some small balm in the few minutes of silent companionship with her friend.

As a wise priest remarked, 'The sense of presence is often of far greater importance than it seems.' To sit beside someone, being fully present, offering compassionate attention can on some occasions be to offer something far more healing than any words could be. This offering of presence can reach the places where words are powerless, and it does a little to redress the present misery of being out of touch with the beloved.

One of my most treasured possessions is a small piece of paper with a short collection of quotations written out on it:

> I looked at the earth, and it was empty and nothing; and at the heavens I saw they had no light. (*Jeremiah 4:23*)

Nothing, nothing, nothing,
Nothing, nothing, nothing,
And even on the mountain nothing.
(St John of the Cross)

These are two of the quotations. They were handed to me without explanation during a period when I was feeling numbed and bleak. I was living in a place of nothingness. Nothing made sense. There was nothing to hold on to, nothing to reach for, nothing to hope for, nothing had worth, there was no point in living. There was nothing except the nothingness which was all around, which was enveloping and invading me. I was isolated by grey nothingness. The person who gave me the piece of paper could not penetrate the nothingness. This piece of paper, however, did seem to be an indication that there were others who had also existed in this ghastly void. And the fact that this person had written out these words gradually seeped through to me as an indication that he too could understand something of this worthless, leaden state. When that tiny fraction of light began infinitely slowly to filter through, I began to feel, almost imperceptibly at first, not quite so numb, not quite so alone.

Depression is an actuality for most people. There is a huge continuum which stretches from being irritable, dejected and out-of-sorts, through desperate and inconsolable sorrow for quite some period as a reaction to loss and bereavement, through weeks on end of hopeless grimness and greyness, to the powerful, forceful downward spiral, which may drive the sufferer into the ward of a psychiatric hospital, or to suicide. Depression holds the sufferer in a grip which makes it seem that ordinary living will be for ever out of reach, where the ordinary realms of contact, communication and comfort are unobtainable. It seems that other people are engaged in life in an impossibly different way. The afflicted person cannot seem to get a handhold to grasp: there seems to be nothing to clutch on to, nothing to help him or her back into mainstream living.

It is frightening and numbing – to the flesh as well as to the spirit – to feel so out of step. It is as if one has become lost on a non-essential byway, while yet realizing that there is, somewhere on the planet, an updated copy of the route map by which others travel, but one has no idea within the darkness shrouding one's living how to find it.

For me when it happened I felt as if I had lost my middle. I had lost that part of me which makes contact with other people. I had lost that infinitely precious core where my inmost feelings and my soul abide. It had disappeared. I felt as if I could not experience anything at gut level. Where I knew I should have feeling, where I should have sensation and sensibility, I was dead. It was at its worst when I was with the people I knew I was normally closest to, because I had no means of communication on any intimate level. In fact I felt I could function on one level only, like a robot programmed simply to engage in the severely practical. I could experience no significance in love, nor any value in being with any of my most beloved relatives. I was anaesthetized, stiff and excluded. The stiffness was fear.

One sufferer who experienced frequent periods of 'black gloomy and certainly hopeless' feelings wrote of it in a little book, *Facing Depression*:[5] 'Perhaps the most acute mental sign is an utter loneliness and desolation which I am not able to describe.' He also writes of the guilt that Christians may be afflicted with: 'Christians ought not to be depressed. Perhaps it is true we ought not to be – but it is no good telling us not to be what we are!' He describes the misery of meaninglessness. He acknowledges he is writing at a time when he is not depressed, that he would be unable to be creative when he was in that kind of darkness, but from this place of relative light he can see a different perspective.

He, like Sheila Cassidy and many others, has found that the words of the Psalmists have resonated deeply when the wracking periods of self-doubt and total worthlessness take hold.

> I am poured out like water, and all my bones are out of joint: my heart also in the midst of my body is even like melting wax.
>
> My strength is dried up like a potsherd, and my tongue cleaveth to my gums: and thou shalt bring me into the dust of the earth. (*Psalm 22:14, 15*)

Save me, O God: for the waters are come in, even unto

my soul. I stick fast in the deep mire, where no ground is: I am come into deep waters, so that the floods run over me. I am weary of crying, my throat is dry: my sight faileth me for waiting so long upon my God. (*Psalm 69:1–3*)

Gonville ffrench-Beytagh writes of the depths of depression bringing one closer to God, who is the basic fact of all being and all existence:

An analogy which helps me personally in thinking of this is the neutron star. This is the kind of star which burns itself out by throwing off its protons and everything else and thus becomes total emptiness, what is called 'infinite gravity', the dead centre, the total stillness at the heart of the whirlpool which yet sucks in everything around it. This, it seems to me, is the epitome of depression and in some ways also a picture of the meaning of the cross. It is to that still centre that depression can bring us.

So, in the hopelessness and meaninglessness and depression, when the guiding beacon of God's glorious transcendence vanishes, it is possible to glimpse the immanence of God 'inside' and to discover that the search for meaning, the search for oneself and the search for God are finally all the same thing. It is in the depths that 'our lives are hid with Christ in God'.

Most people do find that depression, in its most gruelling form, is a self-limiting phase. Most people find it does lift even if only gradually and only to a certain degree. The passing of time, altering circumstances, some kind of better acclimatization, some clearer understanding, or help from the outside which activates a shift within, even physical exertion may help, may relax the tight grim hold of depression. The change may be so slight as to be unnoticeable at the time; there may well be drifts backwards as well as glimpses of distant sunlight. Those glimpses, besides being almost unbearably poignant and painful, can also bring incentive for possible hope during the slow coming-back-to-life and the re-emergence into ordinary daylight, where persons can be recognized and met as fellow pilgrims. The constancy of these fellow pilgrims can be of enormous importance during the struggle, even though the sufferer may feel alienated from them at the time.

Depression is one form of mental illness but 'mental illness' is a term that covers a vast range of degree and type of illness. There are those who seem to have drifted over the brink into 'the land of the fairies' and to be away on their own within some kind of contentment. There are others who are in torment. The feelings of sanity being threatened can create a breeding ground for experiences which may reach terrifying and demonic proportions.

David Reed wrote of agonizing courage, pain, love, beauty and immense struggle, in his book about his wife Anna after her death by suicide in 1973.[6] She had already had several severe breakdowns; at the beginning of another six weeks of psychosis he writes:

> No matter how much I tried to comfort her, to convince her that she need have no fear, she couldn't overcome it [her terror]. She was suddenly convinced that my father – and the CIA – were having us followed . . . the awful pain of witnessing, of experiencing another human being's madness was beginning.

After those incredibly exhausting six weeks there were two days of lucidity and fragile ecstatic happiness before she ran angrily out of the house again. Then he wrote:

> I felt confused, upset, guilty that I'd done something wrong . . . I felt tortured – and upset, disappointed, perhaps even a little fearsome, wondering if I could possibly last out another period of psychosis if it should go to that . . . How could I possibly summon again all the patience, the understanding, the reassurance she needed?

He needed all that, and vast resources of love and tenacity and strength – mental, physical and spiritual – to meet her, and to go on meeting her during these final five weeks of her short life. Through her terrible injuries inflicted by self-immolation, and through her pain, she showed too the great breadth of her spirit: her humour, her concern and her deep love, despite the terrible fears that still pervaded her.

This history of a beautiful, vibrant woman and her husband's love of her is searingly painful to read. It tells of the unbearable strain put upon them both, and of the expenditure – indeed, total draining – of their mental and spiritual resources. In her case actually, and in his case metaphorically, they were stripped to the bone in their long search for integrity, sanity and resolution. Anna had wanted 'to break out of an impossible world'. She had decided to go about it in her own way, and having experienced mental hospitals, drugs and ECT, she wanted to work with a therapist who would not subject her to those kinds of treatment and turn her again into a patient. 'She wanted to find and assert a real self', to find who she really was. Anna was clearly aware that chemical treatment altered something in her integrity as a person, and her battle to find herself became a battle of mortal combat which her physical body was unable to win.

What does happen to the soul when the chemical balance of the brain is altered? This is a question I have been pondering for years and have no answers, only more questions. What happens to the soul when the emotional response to deep loss needs to be tears and gut-level weeping, but anti-depressants have been pumped into the system damming up the tears? Is it the real self that is kept amongst society, functioning with some degree of normality with the help of drugs but with sensitivity and creativity impaired? Or is it the real self who is fragile, vulnerable, but manifestly imaginative and brimming over with originality? And what happens to the soul when the body is busy creating adrenalin through fear, because of the tortures of mental illness?

Ivor Gurney was a patient in the City of London Mental Hospital at Dartford, from December 1922 until his death on St Stephen's Day 1937. These lines from one of his poems speak eloquently and terribly of the torment to the soul:

> And there are orders
> And I am praying for death, death, death,
> And dreadful is the indrawing or outbreathing of breath

Because of the intolerable insults put on my whole soul,
Of the soul loathed, loathed, loathed of the soul.
Gone out every bright thing from my mind.
All lost that ever God himself designed.[7]

Many people find that their well of creativity is reduced to a trickle when mental illness invades. Michael Hurd in his book *The Ordeal of Ivor Gurney*, commenting on Gurney's poems, writes, 'Sometimes the pain is so acute that the outcry can scarcely be held in poetic form . . . in [some examples] the form collapses altogether.' A friend described recently in a letter how she was affected: 'The self becomes shrivelled with fear. A kind of mechanical set of constructs takes over, which erodes creativity, diminishes all spiritual life and makes such heavy demands upon friends that relationships wither and frequently die.' What happens when the burning sensitivity and creativity seem to accelerate too fast and the self goes over that fine edge, the flexible boundary of normality, into something labelled insanity, breakdown, mental illness, which is so excruciatingly painful to the soul?

> I feel that my innermost sanctuary was invaded when I was ill – the very core of my being was under attack and it has left me now feeling that love from outside of me – whether from God, or from friends or from nature – is essential to my survival. The God within, if ever there was such a being, has been harrassed to death. And has not revived.
>
> Any creativity I had has dried up completely. I love looking at pictures, and long for beautiful pictures to look at, but I can't paint any more.

The person who wrote this in a private letter feels now, some months later, that a little creativity has come back, and that the God outside her is more manifest; but she feels off-centre, out of true. Yet in her vulnerability, her apparent brokenness, reliant as she is now on drugs to feel reasonably well, she is a wounded pilgrim who has generously given me much needed space to tend my own meagre spiritual resources.

George Herbert's poem echoes around:

How fresh, O Lord, how sweet and clean
Are thy returns! ev'n as the flowers in spring;

and

Who would have thought my shrivel'd heart
Could have recover'd greennesse? It was gone
Quite underground; . . .

These are thy wonders, Lord of power,
Killing and quickning, bringing down to hell
And up to heaven in an houre;
Making a chiming of a passing bell.
We say amisse,
This or that is:
Thy word is all, if we could spell.[8]

Sometimes our shrivelled hearts do recover some greenness,
but sometimes we cannot recognize where we are, or recollect
any sense in George Herbert's line, 'Thy word is all', as we are
quite unable to spell. It seems that only someone who can
understand and penetrate the isolation, the unconnectedness,
can bring any kind of relief. This is certainly the cry of pain of
Goethe's *Mignon*, the little Italian girl born of an incestuous
union, who dies of homesickness and a broken heart.[9]

Nur wer die Sehsucht kennt	Only one who knows longing
Weiss was ich leide!	Understands what I suffer.
Allein und abgetrennt	Alone and cut off
Von aller Freude	From all joy
Seh'ich ans Firmament	I look up to the firmament
Nach jener Seite.	To the life beyond.

In a Good Friday broadcast, Jim Cotter talking of the cry of
isolation asks 'the darkest question of all':

Am I alone?
I know I have to die alone;
can I face that?

70

is it the end?
In the depths of my loneliness too, I cry,
Am I loved?

A small child
lost among the weeds of a deserted bomb site.

The Psalmist knew the depths of the anguish. The greatest artists seem to have an innate understanding of the dark mysteries of loneliness and death as well as the glorious sublime heights. They are able to speak to the human condition, helping us to bear with the misery as well as pointing us to the joy. Sometimes music can dispel the mental torture as David's cunning playing of his lyre did for Saul (1 Samuel 16:16). Often however it is far more intransigent than that, but in milder, saner interludes it can be a relief to realize that:

At the very centre of the pain
can come a voice that enables you to relax into the pain
and accept the truth of it
that sets you free from its torment.[10]

POSTSCRIPT: Margaret

Margaret called at a suburban vicarage. She has been in and out of psychiatric wards for years. From time to time she calls at the Vicarage and has periods when she makes frequent phone calls, always asking 'Is the Vicar there?' She is sensitive to demands on his time and usually keeps the conversation short. She says what she wants to say and when she has heard sufficient reassurance she rings off. Margaret is terribly afflicted by guilt and is forever frightened that she will not be granted a place in heaven. She is aware that her mental state is not normal and has asked whether mentally ill people can be cured at Lourdes, as she longs to be on a par with everyone else. Often she feels tormented by the devil, and her distress is pitiable. The devil seems to be pulling her by the nose into his domain, and

71

affecting her speaking. At times it is so difficult to understand what she is saying in her distorted nasal voice (which sounds in fact as if her nose is being held and squeezed) that it seems an appallingly daunting task to find any way of consoling her in these waking nightmares, though she seems to find some kind of solace in the church.

This time the Vicar invited her in and they sat together in the kitchen with mugs of tea, and she smoked a cigarette nervously, alternately puffing and quickly sipping. At first her inevitable remarks and questions came up: 'I'm going to heaven.' 'D'you think I'm going to heaven?' 'The devil isn't hurting my nose any more.'

The Vicar asked her when she was going to Walsingham (a shrine for healing in Norfolk) as she had previously told him she would be making a pilgrimage there with a group.

'Tomorrow', she replied, so he asked her if she would light a candle for him.

She turned the conversation to forgiveness, so important for her with her fearful burden of guilt.

'Jesus has forgiven me', she announced in her rapid-fire way of speaking. 'I love everybody. Do you?'

'I try to,' the Vicar replied. 'Sometimes it's not easy.'

They talked of the children at her old school, and the adults too, who had taunted and persecuted her because of her strange appearance and odd manner. The Vicar enquired if she had been able to forgive all these people.

'Yes', she replied, very directly; there was absolute certainty in her response.

The generosity of her soul, which was very apparent during this conversation, is difficult to convey in mere words. Margaret carried on, offering to pray for the Vicar. She trotted out a prayer: 'Lord Jesus, kindle a fire of love in my heart.' 'Perfect love casts out fear,' she added. 'I'll pray for you that you may have love in your heart.' Her simplicity cut right through to her listener. She could have had no knowledge of his complicated spiritual strivings. She would have been unable to follow his theological reasonings and his sophisticated ways of thought. But she had touched him deeply. She had gone straight to the heart of the matter.

Here was one wounded pilgrim ministering to another who had expected to be ministering to her.

The Vicar was stunned and remained still for half an hour, pondering the stark gift which had pierced him to the quick, cutting right through this dividing line between the normal and the abnormal, the giver and the receiver. He had been given what he needed.

> He hath exalted the humble and meek,
> He hath filled the hungry with good things.
> *(Luke 1:52, 53)*

5

AT THE BOTTOM OF THE PILE

And a scribe came up and said to him, 'Teacher, I will
follow you wherever you go'. And Jesus said to him,
'Foxes have holes and birds of the air have nests; but the
Son of Man has nowhere to lay his head'. (*Matthew 8:19,
20*)

From the beginning of my clerical life I was made aware of
homelessness. There was the great, literally ham-fisted Irish-
man, who sat in our back kitchen in Lancashire drinking tea,
and telling us how far he had walked. When I called him a
'long-distance man', he showed me one of his fists and told me
that no one called him that and got away with it. It was an
initiation into one of the many traps for the unwary which lie
in wait for those who work with homeless people.

Then there were a sad couple, teenage parents with two very
small children, who were brought to us by a social worker.
They stayed for a week or two, until accommodation was
found. At first I was struck by their lassitude and their lack of
motivation to do anything, then I realized that this was what
being homeless and at the bottom of the pile meant.

Later, in Manchester, I met the hardened cases, so I thought
– those who seemed to have chosen a homeless way of life,
with temporary accommodation at a Salvation Army hostel or
in a railway arch dedicated to dossers. No one would *choose*
this way of living: it was too risky for one thing, you could at

any time be 'done over' for the bottle in your pocket, or even a packet of fags. At the Cathedral, we had an arrangement with the 'Sally Army' hostel whereby we issued a voucher for a night's accommodation; and for other people, such as ex-prisoners without a job, I had a name and address to whom I could send them. It was little enough, but it was all we could do to help.

Some years later, I went snooping downtown in Norwich. I stopped at an interesting house: overgrown, broken cornices and damaged tiles, cracked flags and smashed windows; but the overall shape was pleasing and it was old, turn of the eighteenth century perhaps. Was the door in the corner open? I picked my way through the elders breaking out in the rough ground which had been a garden and pushed through into the hall. Empty, damp and no furniture at all. I went upstairs: there were signs of habitation, a hole in the centre of the floor ringed with charcoal, and a mattress in the corner. It was sodden with urine.

What had reduced people to living like that? I was to learn in the ensuing years that the reasons included childhood abuse, mental illness, accidents, violence, a host of tragic circumstances and, above all, loss of self-esteem.

As you approach it from any direction, there are proud notices proclaiming 'Norwich – a Fine City'. And so it is, but like any other city you do not have to turn over too many stones to find what is lurking underneath. For all its faults, the church is good at turning over stones. After all it is there, printed in the Anglican Ordering of Deacons (1662 Ordinal), 'And furthermore, it is his office, where provision is made, to search for the sick, poor, and impotent people of the Parish.'

It was a deacon, Colin Slee, who lead the research teams which produced the report *Bedlessness in Norwich*, commissioned by the Current Affairs Research Group of the Norwich Council of Christian Congregations. It received full press publicity and the good burghers of Norwich were shocked to learn that between thirty and fifty people – single homeless[1] – were sleeping rough in the Fine City. Sage heads were shaken over the recommendation that accommodation with a minimum of facilities and supervision should be provided, 'recognizing that the centre would be open to a certain amount of abuse'.

In the summer of 1971, the sunlight slanted past the climbing roses into the study of the Norwich Cathedral Deanery and shone upon two and a half dozen representatives of the 'caring agencies', voluntary and statutory, called together by Alan Webster, the Dean at that time. They were all busy people and no one really wanted the pioneering job implicit in the report. Whether it was the sun, the sandwiches or the glass of wine, no one will ever know, but a small group of people agreed to carry the project forward. There were plenty of redundant churches for accommodation, but the problems were money and personnel, supervision (even minimal) and permission.

The group reached an impasse. With at least three clergymen present, some would say that was a likely result. A social worker said 'The trouble is we haven't enough faith'! We were shamed into action, and on February 7th 1972 the vestry of St James, Pockthorpe (the same church where Frank had learnt the catholic faith from Fr Pitts), squashed between the medieval church and the famous printing firm of Jarrolds, was opened as a Night Shelter, with a capital fund of £250. We had undergone the usual tussle with the authorities, and some good-hearted councillors must have overruled the warnings of the Medical Officer. Permission was given by the health authorities for 7.5 people (sic), because numbers were conditional upon space. There was the £250 in the bank, and an enthusiastic young Norfolkman called Guiseppe willing to manage it five nights a week on a tiny wage. Two nights a week, volunteers staffed it, and I was the back-up if they failed to arrive.

We ran the Shelter in this precarious way until, within a year, we were overrun by dangerously violent itinerant labourers. We closed the Shelter, fitted new locks, built a small office, instituted a new security-conscious regime, and then began again. In the meantime we had made friends with local police (this was always a bone of contention with the Shelter residents), and with several social workers who were relieved the Shelter had opened. We had built up contacts with the psychiatric hospitals and begun to get to know the homeless and rootless population.

The question I most wish to address as we look at the life of the Norwich Night Shelter over the years is, How did we discover hope and meaning and purpose amidst the despair and human degradation? And I suppose that the first answer is that amidst the various horrors there was also great humour, genuine affection and an acceptance of misfortune which was truly humbling and brought forth from the workers a deep commitment to the residents.

A second answer might be that we could see people using the experience of landing 'at the bottom of the pile', and discovering in the generally unappetizing atmosphere of the old Shelter that perhaps they had fallen far enough. When you have arrived at the bottom you can only go up.

The Shelter began as a compassionate response – or even a guilty response – to those bundles of old clothing half-glimpsed from the car as you sped through the shopping centre at night, or went to check if it was indeed a sleeping bag against the wall at the back of C&A as you came out of St Peter Mancroft church after an early weekday service. Perhaps, among those who have been nurtured on heroic Christian stories, such as those of St Vincent de Paul, or even the more recent accounts of Fr Borelli and the *casa delle scugnizzi* (house of orphans) in Naples,[2] there is a desire to emulate and enter what may be seen as the romantic light of the underworld of vagrancy. Those who harbour such dreams are swiftly disabused. There are real terrors, shocking dilemmas and deep despair in working with the homeless.

The most frightening night I spent at the Shelter in the early days (when a volunteer failed to turn up) was marked by a disturbance in the small hours. I was in uneasy slumber on an uncomfortable couch in the passageway adjoining the vestry, when I heard the violent oaths of one of the men (there were no women residents in those days). I went into the sleeping area and turned on the light. I was immediately told, with a wealth of imprecation, to turn it off. The disturber was a big middle-aged man with a record for grievous bodily harm (GBH), and the cause of the upset was revealed by the spreading patch of damp in the middle of his trousers. He had wet himself and was moving to dry off his trousers at the gas fire by the wall. I refused to turn out the light until all was settled once more. The man picked up a metal chair and swung it over his head to strike. I braced myself for the blow, for there was no room to dodge, but to my surprise it never fell. After further cursing, calm descended and we all went back to sleep. But I had been scared, and it was a long time before my heart reduced to its normal beats. Years later, other workers experienced much more frightening scenes, with vicious fights in the Shelter, often mercifully resolved by the other residents pulling the fighters apart. There has been a stabbing or two, though it is a rare occasion when the police are called, at least for incidents inside the Shelter.

One of the many dilemmas faced by the Night Shelter workers was created by a man with psychiatric problems. There is a high incidence of homeless people in this category.[3] One such man used to mumble to himself in the evenings in the old St James' vestry. Eventually the worker managed to hear what he was saying: 'I only want one, just one . . . just one child.' After gentle questioning, a shock of horror went through the worker as he established that the man seemed to want to kill a child, just one, and he would be satisfied. It would be easy to dismiss such talk as crazed raving, but once you have made contact with such a disturbed person, it seems irresponsible to do nothing. So we set about finding out what we could do. Horrifying though it may seem, it transpired that the psychiatric hospital authorities could not act until the man in question actually took action himself. There was no preventive way. Fortunately, the man did nothing and eventually disappeared.

One local homeless character seemed to me the epitome of despair. Peter wore an overcoat done up with a safety pin in all weathers. He was an educated man and could read French, and for years the Presbyterian minister provided him with both English and French books. He had long straggly unwashed hair and beard, a moustache bearing heavy evidence of his frequent colds, and a pinched face peering out through round glasses. His complete worldly possessions were packed into three or four plastic bags. He would come into the Shelter for a cup of tea, but could not be persuaded to stay the night. After one such attempt to coax him in, he walked off into the rain coming down in torrents, and as he went I heard him weeping. One could only guess at the inner fears which held him so tightly and at the despair which bowed him down. He hated being clean, but from time to time he became a health hazard not only to himself but to others and it was certainly advisable to stand upwind of him. We would call in a social worker and off he went to a hospital or the Public Health Centre to be given a bath. Once, he got his own back by squeezing out a whole tube of delousing ointment on the stairs leading up to the bathroom. After many years, and several winters of severe bronchial illness, Peter was persuaded to accept a council flat; but, to my knowledge, he never spent a whole night at the Shelter.

It was not long before the vestry was overcrowded. To keep on the right side of the law, we were turning away far too many people as the Shelter became an acceptable refuge to people who had not dared to trust it to begin with. The logical step was to move into the church itself, after removing the pitchpine pews, thus giving us first of all a maximum of fifteen bedspaces on wooden floors, and later, when the whole of the church was occupied, forty-five spaces. Toilet facilities were limited, so we were required to supply an elsan toilet, conveniently situated next to a seventeenth-century memorial to one Mr Chambers. Second-hand rubberized mattresses were obtained from a hospital at minimal cost, and after one rather cold winter, a sponsored fast by the young people of a suburban church provided us with the money for a splendid second-hand heater with the necessary ducting. Occasionally there were public protests about the Shelter and its occupants, but no one ever made a serious complaint about our use of this ancient sacred building. Rather, there was a widespread sense of approval that the church was being used 'christianly', to provide shelter for the homeless.

After a couple of years, the Shelter was more financially sound, with a securer relationship with the then DHSS. We were able to employ a part-time worker in addition, and volunteers became more reliable. The job of a night shelter worker requires a high degree of acceptance of strangeness, even bizarreness, of character and an instinctive understanding of psychological damage. Such people are rare and often have an unusual life experience themselves. One such, John, became our worker, having been a resident for several weeks. He made himself useful around the place, understood the problems, including the complex relationship with the DHSS (who helped us a great deal, despite being vilified as the 'Department of Stealth and Total Obscurity'). So, when our senior member of staff moved on, John was a natural candidate for the job. Our chairman was concerned because John hinted at a criminal past but would not give details. We trusted him, gave him the job, and he proved himself an excellent senior worker, with a deep understanding of the residents. Surely he was one of the wounded healers himself.

Another assistant worker came from among the numbers of the residents. Tony was a very unhappy man and had run away from his home, wife and children the other side of the country. He was duly appointed when a vacancy occurred, and lived – probably quite illegally – in the priest's room over the porch, drawing up the ladder after him at night. He was very capable and made many improvements both to the premises and to the lives of the residents. Eventually, after the chairman of the committee made contact with Tony's family, he was reconciled with them and left us.

After some years, we realized that St James was an unsatisfactory building for the care of homeless people: it was expensive to maintain and difficult to keep clean, especially when there was an outbreak of lice. I remember one day calling at the church and looking across the interior through a cloud of white dust: the Health Department was delousing the place. In 1976 the Historic Churches Trust provided us with St Martin-at-Oak in Oak Street which had been converted into a church hall. We had it divided into cubicles, to give a little more privacy to residents. A similar number could be accommodated and the longer-term residents had beds in the former chancel. There were better washing facilities and a kitchen, which was eventually improved, to provide breakfast and an evening meal.

By 1979, we had three full-time and two part-time workers, and the organization was beginning to settle into a regular pattern of provision for residents. We wrestled with the constant problems of a common life-style involving vagrancy, collapse, temporary Night Shelter accommodation, and, for some people, ejection, following seriously anti-social behaviour such as violence and drunkenness. Often valuable progress could be made into a supported tenancy in one of the 'Bridge Houses'. But the staff often have the impression that they can only help a little and may only postpone tragedy, despite the fact that the provision is varied and can respond to a number of differing needs of quite damaged and disturbed people.

There is no typical Night Shelter resident, but the story of Ernest shows a progress through successive tragedies in and out of the Shelter. He was about twenty years old, in a scruffy suit, with piercing dark eyes and dirty teeth. He was a student drop-out from a Midlands University and there was more than a suspicion of drug abuse. The staff discussed the possibility of a move for him after he had been around for about a year. Nothing seemed possible or likely.

Then a new worker was taken on, a young woman with some experience in work with the homeless. Ernest fell in love with her. It turned out that she was unhappily married to an alcoholic, and was pleased to reciprocate his attention. She obtained a divorce and they married. Ernest became clean and tidy and found a responsible job as a security officer at a large factory. They had two children. Then one day Ernest discovered his wife was having an affair with his brother and he went to pieces. He came back to the Night Shelter, and the last time I saw him was outside Leicester railway station, where he was on his way to a work rehabilitation centre for a training course.

We entertained hopes for Ernest, and his life may not always be blighted by his experiences. But that may never be the case for the following two people: baby-faced Jim and the colourful Thomas.

Jim did not have a good start in life: his mother was a prostitute and his father was her father and therefore his grandfather. At the age of four he was taken into 'care' by the Social Services. The reason seemed to be that his mother's life-style was harmful to him; but it is interesting that his sister born a year later was not taken into care, and has since grown up without any major problems. In the next seven years Jim lived in five different Children's Homes. The only other friend he ever had during this time was another boy of similar age. Because the workers felt that this was a homosexual relationship, they were parted.

Jim was fostered at the age of eight by an elderly working-class couple whose own child had grown up and left home. The foster father regularly assaulted Jim sexually and when he objected he was locked up in a cupboard for many hours. Jim thought this was the norm, so he never complained. Eventually this was discovered by his doctor and the boy was removed. The foster father went to prison for three years.

The intelligence and artistic skill which Jim possessed help the Social Services to interest another pair of foster parents, also elderly. They were a retired professional couple living in a large country house. So, at the age of twelve, Jim started a new life with a totally new set of values and customs to learn. He made a good, even loving, relationship with his foster father, but unfortunately he died three years later, and Jim was partly blamed for it by the foster mother. He endured a worsening situation but as soon as he could he left – at the age of sixteen. A few days later, he arrived at the Night Shelter. I knew Jim when he was developing his 'baby-faced conmanship ploy': he would approach benign looking people after church on Sunday with a Bible under his arm, tell them a story, probably partly based on this appalling childhood, and relieve them of a few banknotes. He was persuaded to stop this. After bouts of drink and drug abuse which threatened both his health and life, Jim, now in his thirties, is in one of the Trust's supported group homes, and still grappling with the dreadful legacy of his past.

Thomas's story is quite different. One bright sunny day, I drove along the dual carriageway in the city. As I drew up to the traffic lights, I noticed this man I knew wearing yellow boots and carrying two black plastic sacks, balancing an empty bottle on his head and singing at the top of his voice. When Thomas is like this, he is banned from the Shelter, because he is totally out of control and badly disturbs the other residents. For periods he is sober. Then he is a model resident, busying himself with writing incoherent and interminable pages in capital letters about his life. One day he is a Christian, the next he calls himself Mohammed, and provides a labyrinthine explanation.

Before Thomas came to the Shelter, he was a mild-mannered and respectably employed citizen in one of Norfolk's pleasant small towns. One day the local butcher picked an argument with him, lost his temper and struck him with a cleaver. Resulting brain damage has left him disturbed, obsessive and prey to the drink. His obsessiveness has led him to the bizarre practice of filling his boots and rubber gloves with water. Nobody quite knows why, nor why he is not in a mental hospital. He is one of the many who 'does not fit', except, perhaps, at the bottom of the pile.

It is a quarter to eight in the evening, there is a thud on the door (the bell has been ignored for some reason), and 'The Mighty Atom', who is on duty, goes to answer it. Thomas, clean but drunk, looks down on this diminutive woman, who smiles at him and says 'Come in, how are you?' She has to decide best how to deal with him, whether he will have to go – depending how the drink takes him – or whether she will make an attempt to remove his boots and rubber gloves and try to anoint his extremities with the special ointment which has been prepared for him. Tonight he becomes noisy and The Mighty Atom has the difficult task to persuade him to leave. How she does it, I do not know, but the task is eventually accomplished and nothing is broken.

Later that night, there is a disturbance outside, voices are raised, the worker on duty wonders whether to ring the police. When it is obvious she must, it is too late, the damage has started. Seventy-six of the small diamond-shaped panes in the windows are shattered by a metal rod in the hands of a former resident. The immediate suspect is Thomas, but no, that is not his typical behaviour, and days later a known troublemaker is discovered as the likely culprit. It is a waste of time bringing charges, for he would never be able to pay. By the grace of God, a local glazier does the job within a week and 'forgets' to send the bill. It is all very chaotic, all very irregular, but through it all shines the glory of God, mostly covered up with grime. Attentive people catch glimpses.

When I have spoken to church and other groups about this

work, I frequently receive the response 'Oh, you do such *worth-while* work!' But for those who run the Shelter, it is a constant struggle against the despair which runs into the soul when people like Ernest and Jim come back again and again. Are the cards stacked against such people? Do they bring such disaster upon themselves? The individualist theory of personal responsibility would have us believe this, but as I look upon the residents and consider their life stories, such as I know of them, I cannot accept this simplistic explanation. I become angry, and dare even to believe it is righteous anger, when I hear, as I once did, a leader of the County Council saying that if he found a tramp in the gutter he would leave him there. All that is necessary for evil to triumph is that good people should do nothing. We may not be able to prevent the tragedy of an Ernest, but we do have it within our power to alleviate his lot.

Like a spider in the middle of its web, aware of activity on the periphery and anywhere along the threads, sits Chris Roberts, the Chief Executive of the Trust. He oversees the operation and picks up the crises and problems when they escalate. His philosophy is obscure and agnostic, yet resting in parts of the Christian tradition, a natural compassion, and in the wisdom of contemporary science and psychology. Years ago we fought the battle with those who wanted to insist on 'Christian' workers. Often our specifically Christian workers have fallen by the wayside: 'God is honoured by a dentist being a good dentist, not by his singing hymns.'[4] Collaboration between those with different insights is often the secret of the success of the Trust.

'Night Shelter' has become much more than a temporary roof over the head of homeless people. It is now St Martin's Housing Trust; there are six group homes and a cluster unit, each of which has the support of a weekly visit from one of the staff, and there is Carrow Hill House (started 1982), a permanent home for twenty-two of those who are unable to cope with life 'outside' in the community. There is also a custom-built Night Shelter, St Martin's House, opened in 1990, which accommodates thirty-eight people, and the old Shelter at St Martin-at-Oak still houses a maximum of twenty-four, thus, a total of 112 otherwise homeless people can be looked after. The whole organization is now much more like a therapeutic community, and close attention is paid to understanding the residents as human beings as well as meeting their immediate basic human needs for food, warmth, shelter and clothing. It has links with Ferry Cross, a separate charity which cares for up to fifty people with alcohol and related problems. The original Ferry Cross was a detoxification and treatment house for up to eight people with drink problems (started 1979).

The Trust could not function without institutional compassion, expressed through the understanding of the Norwich Historic Churches Trust and the Norwich City Council, who are the landlords. The latter, as the Housing Authority, has also been the main 'broker' through which the finance has been channelled to enable the development to occur. Other essential finance comes through the generosity of the churches and individuals in the community. So the struggle to combat despair at the bottom of the pile has to take place at both personal and institutional levels.

Chris Roberts and I tried to uncover the difference between our views of the work of the Trust. Mine was an optimistic, more hopeful view of the work, believing that many of the exceedingly damaged people who came to the Shelter could be helped and could make their way towards a safer, more satisfactory life. Chris had a gloomy view, suggesting that most of our residents are always going to be there, are always going to be the butts of society, living painful, tortuous lives right to the end. We agreed that every small success the Trust achieved was a boon: 'There is more joy in heaven over one sinner that repents.' But we seem, he suggested, to have reached a point in human development which is characterized by extremes of life-style, extremes of character, which causes the underclass to exist in tragedy and unhappiness. Chris wrote: 'The despair felt by the residents is usually hidden and often a jovial face is presented to the world, but it isn't far away and comes to the surface in private conversations.' He thought it would take centuries for human beings to understand commitment to each other and to the planet in such a measure that would render the work of the Trust unnecessary. 'My fear is that despite the increasing tolerance shown by many people, "the enemies without" grow no weaker and probably never will.' For me, this is where the personal care of the Trust becomes political, and I look to those who take responsibility for the good ordering of our society to develop visions for the future which will encourage the values of commitment to people and planet rather more than essentially insensitive power games.

POSTSCRIPT: On the fear of the enemy

Fear:

> of the tramp at the door; of what demands he might make of me;
>
> of the proposal to build a hostel for ex-psychiatric patients next door; of their leering faces and strange behaviour;
>
> of the drunken homeless woman in the street;
>
> that we may be invaded by a foreign power or taken over by a people with an alien culture;
>
> that if we do not maintain the status quo, the change will be for the worse.

We must be careful. We must defend ourselves. We must defend our society, to which wealth and technology have brought so much.

Our society: television, cars, computers, microchips, electronics. Our society, with its hospitals, its welfare state, its design and high fashion. Our society, where there is caring and vandalism, compassion and rape; where there is love and mugging; where there is sensitive care and drug-trafficking and cult-idolatry; where there is generosity and Live Aid and take-away food and hooliganism and class-consciousness and unemployment; where there is warmth and affection and racism and sexism and greed and poverty. Our society, our consumer society, our throw-away society, where we strive to do what is best for our children, and often remain immune to the plight of the disabled, the handicapped, the elderly, the despairing, the dying, and their immense struggles and the immense struggles of those who care for them. Our society: them and us.

There is much that is good – overwhelmingly good – that happens daily: we see it in the seemingly small occurrences, like the smile of a baby, the care of a shop assistant, the pleasure of an old man as a child takes his hand, the transient whiteness of the new convolvulus by the roadside; we see it in the devotion of our real friends when we are in trouble, and in the delight of teenagers volunteering to help children with special needs. There is much that is amazingly beneficial in our technology: there is speed of delivery and availability of information; there are many laborious tasks now accomplished by machines; because of advances in medicine, our four-year-old son survived peritonitis and flourishes; a hundred years ago he would have died.

But behind it all, behind progress, behind improvement and always behind people, there is the possibility for good and the possibility for evil.

Behind affluence is the fear that something may rob us of security. It is part of the same continuum of fear which begins in poverty, with the fear that we may not be able even to survive.

Behind fear there lurk both apathy and evil, which push us into defending ourselves against our perceived enemy and drive us to take measures to destroy that enemy.

But who is our enemy? John Donne wrote:

> I have a sinne of feare, that when I've spunne
> My last thred, I shall perish on the shore;[5]

I have a sin of fear too: a nameless, dark fear which prevents me from even spinning that last thread. It paralyses me into inaction so that I am unable to take the steps I could to remedy or alleviate the danger of the situation. Perhaps it is the fear of my freedom to accept responsibility; if I decide to use my power I shall have to brace myself for the consequences, which may take me into further action and further danger. Perhaps it is the fear of facing my inadequacies: although I may have the capacity to act, I may very possibly be confronted with failure. Surely it would be better for my self-image not to try, rather than face disappointment and humiliation.

87

Or would it? Of the Suffering Servant, Isaiah wrote 'He was despised and rejected of men.' Of whom was he thinking as he wrote?

St Paul wrote to the Philippians (2:8) that Christ Jesus 'humbled himself, and in obedience accepted even death – death on a cross', the ultimate, despicable failure of the death of a common criminal.

I am not made of such metal. My fear wins. My courage fails me. Perhaps my fear is that I may be wrong – wrong even before I begin; I am frozen into total lethargy.

Other people may have fears which drive them into frenzied activity, so that they are prevented from having the time to stand still and face the true cause of the fear. I, too, fear the truth of looking honestly at another person's point of view: they have their reasons for thinking that way, but if I dare to examine those reasons they may rock my security. If I were to be honest, I might have to alter my watertight argument; my perceptions of right-wing, left-wing, the balance of power, the economy, the government may seem to be swimming and struggling for survival. Even that most frail and precious stronghold, the perception of myself, will be struggling if I alter my position. Maybe I shall indeed 'perish on the shore'.

The sin of fear is that this is the all and nothing of my existence; there is nothing beyond the limited horizon of myself. And this self is hollow: in the hollow of my being I am gripped by the fear that I am ultimately unacceptable and unlovable.

St Francis of Assisi, after night-long vigils, seemed to emerge from terrible battles, as if he had been violently beaten during his prayers, fighting with the enemies of his soul.[6] Most of us cannot attain to his sanctity, which enabled him to find great joy and serenity. Perhaps, though, I can begin to look at the enemy of fear within me. Perhaps I can begin to acknowledge it as part of my muddled, yearning self, before I ride out on my charger having conquered my lethargy to do battle with the enemy without.

For there are, very certainly, enemies without. The enemies which cause the evils of homelessness, hunger, sickness and loneliness are myriad. There are enemies born of laziness and weakness and ignorance, and there are enemies born of cruelty and destructiveness. Some of these are blatantly apparent in their madness, such as the destruction of Thomas's mind. Some of the evil is insidiously disguised, like some governmental cuts in benefits and the introduction of the Social Fund, which are supposed to counter the evils of the waste of money caused by the abuse of the system, but which in fact cause further hardship, often to innocent, needy people already caught in the evil of poverty.[7]

We are bidden to love our enemies, to love them, in John Dalrymple's phrase, with 'initiative and fidelity'. We are more likely to bring down the enemy without successfully if we can allow a surrender of the enemy within to the love of God.

Only a God who suffers as Christ suffered, even to death, is sufficient for the suffering that is taking place in our society and in our world. Nothing less could have any claim on our love.

John Donne's poem concludes radiantly,

> But sweare by thy selfe, that at my death thy sonne
> Shall shine as he shines now, and heretofore;
> And having done that, Thou hast done,
> I feare no more.

With that kind of faith and love, it is possible to begin to conquer the enemy.

6

SUDDEN DEATH

There is a refrain which keeps returning to me when thinking about sudden death. It is David's lament for the loss of his son:

> O my son Absalom, my son, my son Absalom! would God I had died for thee, O Absalom, my son my son! (*2 Samuel 18:33*)

This anguished piercing agony must have been deeply felt by Thomas Weelkes, an organist of Winchester Cathedral, who died in his late forties in 1623. I don't know whether he had lost a child, but his anthem, 'When David heard that Absalom was slain', has harsh dissonances, deeply expressive of the pain of David's loss, and is very advanced for the music of that time. It had not been all plain sailing for David with his very handsome son, and Absalom's death occurred during a battle skirmish between them, yet David reeled in his grief.

The cry 'Would God I had died for thee' is the forerunner of many such cries; it lies at the heart of parents' protective love of their children. It lies at the centre of the agony of watching a beloved suffer. I see this at the hospice where I work, where husbands and wives are keeping a loving vigil at the bedside of their dying spouse. I know that some of them are wishing desperately that they could change places with their partner and suffer the cancer in their stead. And that cry is in the aching impotence of recognizing that nothing will bring the dead back to life.

In her book *In the Beginning*[1] Irina Ratushinskaya writes: 'I know from personal experience that it is much easier to go into prison yourself than to see others taken.' She recognizes the torture experienced by those who watch but can do nothing as their friends disappear, knowing that they may never emerge alive. In a similar vein, she remarks 'It is much more humiliating to have to tolerate filth than to clean it up.' Perhaps that lies at the bottom of the never-ending search for truth, for justice, for compensation, for recognition of all the suffering involved, for the grief-stricken relatives of those who have died in sudden disasters, for whom life is now just a mess.

For the relatives there is living with 'the neverness that is so painful. Never again to sit with us at table . . . all the rest of our lives we must live without him. Only our death can stop the pain of his death. A month, a year, five years – that I could live with. But not this forever.'[2] For people separated by sudden disaster there is no chance of saying what needed to be said, no chance of a message, no chance of making up after cross words, no chance of saying 'I love you', nor even 'Goodbye'. There is no chance ever of acting on the regrets.

For people separated from a person or persons by sudden death, where there is no forewarning of the calamity with its trail of raw messy chaos, the grief they have to come to terms with is compounded with the shock of the impact. This shock can ricochet against every conceivable aspect of life, leaving nothing untouched. The dire malevolence which has extinguished all hope, all joy, all normality in such a short moment can leave the bereaved feeling entirely cut off from their own humanity, as if the body itself has been amputated from its own life source.

This is how it seemed to feel for the parents of two teenage boys crushed to death with many others in an appalling accident. The anguish of these people, exacerbated as it has been by delays in legal processes, as well as the necessarily painstaking collection of evidence by police investigators, seems to have isolated them in their grief and alienated them from all hope.

For months the only thing which seemed clear was the extreme tension in which they were living, because it seemed that every moment their gaping and excruciatingly painful wounds were hurt afresh. Then there was the further deep shock which undid all the minor healings, when the police inquiry began seven months later amidst quantities of amassed evidence. The oft repeated words 'It should never have happened' were their refrain after the meeting with the police, and at both the informal and formal inquests which followed. In some grotesque fashion, this inner anguish seemed to transform their beings into something akin to the pillar of salt which had once been Lot's wife (Genesis 19:26).

The inquests were long delayed in coming. The informal inquest was set up by the coroner fifteen months after the deaths, and the parents were invited to attend. They were, in the event, unable to face this, but watched the proceedings on a TV monitor in a remote room away from the court. The formal inquest six months later was a long drawn out affair. The parents attended several sessions, which were usually pronounced by them to have been a waste of time, and when months later the verdict came – that no one was to blame – their bitterness was palpable, and the more so for being half expressed and half suppressed. It is as if the father's bitter prophecy, 'It'll never be any different. I'll always feel the same', voiced early on after the death of the two lads, was self-fulfilling. And the mother's panic attacks, breathlessness and shivers continued.

Have these parents allowed all hope to die? Or do they sense that any glimmer of hope would somehow betray their boys' memory? Perhaps as yet, many months later, it is too soon to know.

> What is it that makes the death of a child so indescribably painful? I buried my father and that was hard. But nothing at all like this. One expects to bury one's parents; one doesn't expect – not in our day and age – to bury one's children. The burial of one's child is a wrenching alteration of expectations.
>
> But it's more than that. I feel the more but cannot speak it. A child comes into the world without means of sustenance. Immediately we parents give it of our own . . . We take it on ourselves to stay with this helpless infant all the way so that it has a future, a future in which we can delight in its delight and sorrow in its sorrow. Our plans and hopes and fears are plans and hopes and fears for it . . .

That future which I embraced to myself has been destroyed. He slipped out of my arms. For twenty-five years I guarded and sustained and encouraged him with these hands of mine, helping him to grow and become a man of his own. Then he slipped out and was smashed.[3]

There is this sickening, wrong, upside-downness of the death of a child while its parents are still alive, written of so eloquently here by Nicholas Wolterstorff, in which all investments in the future seem to have died with the child. For the parents of the two boys, losing not one child but their whole family in one single tragic incident, the shock must be akin to the shock of burns, affecting the whole metabolism of the body. They suffered the shock of their boys' death, and with it the horrifying nature of their death, like a nightmare that will always be with them. Such terrible wounds take a long, long time to heal.

All grief is shocking. Many newly bereaved people feel numbed by the shock. Often neither the pain of the loss, nor the ordinary needs for food and sleep get translated into action. Or a sort of mechanical process may take over, totally anaesthetizing the unbearable wounds and the intensity of the ache. This is protective and necessary: if the full impact of the pain were felt at once, the bereaved person might find the strain utterly intolerable. There are indeed many instances of bereaved spouses dying of 'broken hearts', suffering a coronary thrombosis, or developing arterio-sclerotic heart disease. How often it is said 'I feel as if half of me is gone'. Grief is shocking to outsiders too. The horror of death can seem to onlookers to have tainted those who are bereaved, so that they 'pass by on the other side', or have little tolerance for the expression of grief, chastising those who weep, because the deceased 'wouldn't like it'. Many widows and widowers say 'I have found out who my friends are', because so many acquaintances cannot cope with the extreme feelings which surface with the turbulent waves of grief.

In some sense, almost every death has a startling suddenness about it. Even when illness has been sapping energy and vitality, and death is the inevitable and expected outcome, there is a Rubicon crossed at the moment of dying, and thereafter a yawning enormity of difference in a world which is now the less by one of its inhabitants. Even when death has come gradually and peacefully there is a strangeness, an unfamiliarity about the very surroundings, where once, only a moment previously, the person was living and breathing in his or her own place on earth. Now there is an emptiness, a quietly gaping void.

With sudden death, there is the added horror of the senselessness and the subsequent raging against that senselessness, the coming to terms with what seems to be a gigantic and malicious hoax, a terrible mistake, which has to be accommodated as the tragedy that in truth it really is. That which simply cannot be has happened.

'My grief rose and rose and rose. Like a rocket in the sky it arched; it burst into a thousand diamond ice-like particles of horror that splintered all over the ground of my being – many are not yet thawed.'[4] So wrote a father after the death of his quicksilver eleven-year-old daughter who had been killed in a road accident.

I became closely involved with another little girl who had been conceived some years later against all the medical odds. She was carried to term, while those of us closest to her mother held our breath: so much can happen during those weeks while the tiny life in the womb is quickening and developing. The date she was due to be born came and went. Fourteen days passed and there were tinges of anxiety. There was no sign of her mother going naturally into labour, and so her birth was induced. It seemed that somehow this little baby could not arrive without artificial help and she was welcomed into the world a trifle over-cooked. But to her mother her birth was truly miraculous. She had never doubted that within her she carried a girl child, and now little Anna Catherine was here: the daughter she had feared she would never be able to have. She was ecstatic.

Birth is always miraculous, with the delicate latency hidden within the immature wholeness of the tiny body of an infant; Anna Catherine, whose mother had relinquished all hopes of natural motherhood, was doubly loved and welcomed. I saw her (against the hospital rules!) when she was less than twelve hours old, tiny and perfect despite marks on her head from the

forceps, and fingernails which had needed trimming immediately because of her overlong stay inside her mother. She had
a mop of dark hair, which quickly began to turn a blondy red.
For mother and baby the beginning is a time of sensitivity, of
newness, a time for becoming acquainted with each other in an
unique way: Anna Catherine was learning to suckle and her
mother's joy knew no bounds. I saw them at the beginning of
a very close emotional bonding which had, in other ways,
begun nine months ago. From the moment mother and daughter caught sight of each other, it was apparent that they already
knew each other intimately.

Anna Catherine's mother felt an undreamt of contentment.
She experienced a peace she had never known before. Everything had fallen into place and she felt within her a deep delight
which had a strength of its own. She was a single mother who
had her own place in a large, warm, loving family, many
members of which had come through their own tribulations
(and whose warmth and sensitivity have been there for me,
too, when I needed it). She never doubted the rightness of the
gift of Anna Catherine. She knew that to bring up her child
single handed was no easy matter, but she felt well supported,
and carried with her the steady conviction that together she and
Anna Catherine 'could do it'.

Anna Catherine grew, as babies do. She was surrounded with
love, and her mother, though often tired, never felt anywhere
near an irritable breaking point, even during the nights when
the baby was unable to settle. Anna Catherine learnt to smile
early, she seemed to know her mother with a clarity and an
awareness that was beautiful to behold. She was full of vitality
– she loved living, and was most assuredly and fully herself.

She was born in midsummer, and the light sunniness of the
world seemed to be mirrored in her. If unconditional love is
the prerequisite for nurturing a human being's potential, then
everything was in Anna Catherine's favour: she had everything
going for her, and she thrived.

In September she travelled with mother and grandmother to
Ireland for a glorious holiday. It was a delight to see them so
happy when they came to visit us with the holiday snaps soon
after.

There are many photographs of her, one for almost every day of her short life. For her life ended inexplicably at the beginning of October.

Her mother woke early on a Saturday morning to see immediately that something was desperately wrong with the warm little body lying beside her. Anna Catherine was dead.

She was a victim of that infinitely tragic and puzzling syndrome, Sudden Infant Death, or cot death. The post mortem revealed no information, no evidence of why she had stopped breathing. There had been no trauma for her. There was no mark on her. In death she looked tranquil and contented. It seemed unbelievable.

How could it be that this laughing, happy, vivacious, so-much-wanted little girl had been cut short so prematurely at fourteen weeks? Her mother was in a state of total shock. And her mother's mother, who had known so much bereavement herself, felt more keenly affected by this death than by any other.

I had been one of the first to know of Anna Catherine's conception, had been honoured to greet her within hours of her arrival in this world, and now exactly one hundred days later, I was with the family within hours of her death.

The serenity and the joy she had brought to her mother, the rightness, and the feeling of everything coming together for good that her mother had experienced, were all now shattered. Now there was something profoundly, hideously awry.

There is nothing that can be said that will bring any balm or any comfort to this sort of grief. The bitter lamentations of Rachel weeping for her children 'because they are not' (Matthew 2:18) are reiterated by every mother when her child is no more.

Anna Catherine's mother said 'it seemed wrong even to do the necessary ordinary things, like going to the loo', in the face of such catastrophe. Nothing ordinary had any place beside this event of such earth-shaking, sickening import. Nothing seemed to make sense. Nothing seemed to carry any significance. She was trembling with her whole body, but could not weep or rage. In one juddering moment, all that was light had been blacked out, all that was warmth and movement and joy had been turned cold as stone and wiped out.

96

When Anna Catherine died her mother's whole self was yearning for her. Her arms were empty when they should have been enfolding that trusting little body who nestled closely into her: her breasts were filling with milk which Anna Catherine should have been suckling for comforting nourishment: everything in her was in full sail, set to nurture her little daughter – her voice to encourage and console, her hands to protect, to help and to guide. Now there was nothing but an empty, deeply aching, discordant void.

I remembered John Taylor's passage in *Weep not for me*:

> I was asked by a friend to visit a young couple whose two year old daughter had been found dead in her cot. They were still stunned and haunted by the old question Why?, and sometimes Why her? I simply could not offer them the conventional reassurance about it all being in God's providence, a mystery now but one day to be seen as part of a loving plan . . . I said to them instead that their child's death was a tragic accident, an unforeseeable failure in the functioning of the little body: that, so far from being willed or planned by God, it was for him a disaster and a frustration of his will for life and fulfilment, just as it was for them, that God shared their pain and loss and was with them in it.[5]

A week later, on a beautiful, warm clear day, Anna Catherine's mother carried with quiet composure the little coffin into church for the funeral. Anna Catherine's uncle read these words by John Taylor, and many, many people, whose lives had been touched by Anna Catherine in her short sunny life were present, out of love for her and love for her mother.

Anna Catherine would have been eighteen months old now: she would have been trying out her talking skills with her devastating charm: she would have been reaching and exploring and walking and finding all manner of heaven-sent situations to investigate. But for her mother the pain is never-ending.

Of course, Anna Catherine's mother did not stay for ever completely at a standstill, static in her grief. Later, she was interviewed on the local radio about Sudden Infant Death Syndrome. She organized some fund-raising and found a new job where she is able to use her very considerable abilities for the benefit of others in difficulties. But the pain is still there.

The anger and grief that this death should have happened remain with her. Sometimes they can be drowned out by business, by involvement and activity, but then they surface unannounced with sharp intensity that does not seem to lessen with the passage of time. Paradoxically, at the same time, she needs to keep the memories of Anna Catherine vivid and alive. Thank God for those photographs, which revive the sensations of Anna Catherine's closeness, the feeling of her fresh skin at bath time, her smell; and thank God for those memories which are more than memories – the conviction that she held when Anna Catherine was with her, that 'together we can do it'.

I suppose the marvel for me is the way Anna Catherine's mother and grandmother, despite (or because of?) the episodes of deep tragedy in their lives, devote their time to 'suffering humanity', and, as their many friends will testify, are such pleasure to be with. Always there is the funny side of life to be enjoyed and affectionately giggled over. In their company, life, even as wounded pilgrims, seems a worthwhile pilgrimage. Although the pain is so harsh for Anna Catherine's mother, it is still infinitely better to risk living and loving, and not for one second does she regret having loved and lived with Anna Catherine. When I asked Anna Catherine's mother, very tentatively, if I could include something about Anna Catherine in this book, she replied gently, 'Anything, if it will help in any way'.

From my own experience, I believe that the healing of emotional pain involves forgiveness. Perhaps all healing involves forgiveness. Who or what is to be forgiven is not always clear. Ursula Fleming, in her book *Grasping the Nettle*,[6] describes a method of relaxing and dispersing pain so that it is coped with by the whole body. She writes of mental pain as well as physical pain, saying 'If you are bereaved, you FEEL the loss, you don't just think about it.' She goes on:

> There has to be an element of forgiveness in this. When a part of the body stops functioning, is injured and in pain,

we treat it as an enemy, a traitor of the whole. It is frightening so we imprison it behind a barrier of tension . . . When
you relax you accept and forgive your treacherous body.

Stephen Verney, in his profound and thought-provoking
book *Water into Wine*, wrote two chapters towards the end
called 'Life through Death'. He writes: 'Forgiveness summarizes
the whole work of Jesus which John has described in a series
of images.'[7] These different ways of describing forgiveness offer
'a new vision, and they set people free to see themselves and
everybody else in a new light'. Forgiveness is about letting go
and about new freedom.

Though it is very hard, I think that maybe the only way of
finding life through death is through this letting go: letting go,
so that there is a change of heart and mind. It is 'both adventuring out into something totally new, and coming back home to
something profoundly old'[8] – seeing life exactly as it was before
but somehow without the encumbrances that keep life chained
so that movement is well nigh impossible. It is only a shift as
big and daring as letting go that will enable fresh shoots to
pierce through the heavy, claggy, remorseless ground of death.

When there has been death by a sudden tragedy it is often
very difficult to forgive. How can a parent let go of the anger
towards a murderer? How can a husband forgive a drunken
driver for killing his wife? How can the grieving relatives of
the Hillsborough disaster forgive the police? How can those left
mourning after the sinking of the *Herald of Free Enterprise* forgive the men who failed to close the ferry doors? How can the
Jews forgive the Nazis for the genocide inflicted on their race?
Once, when Frank (see chapter 3) was staying with us, a Nazi
war criminal was being tried in Israel. There seemed to be a
tremendous baying for the blood of this man, but Frank pen-
sively remarked that we who had not suffered from this man's
cruelty had neither the power nor the right to expect or even
to ask the persecuted to forgive him. Only those who are
suffering can do that.

Archbishop Anthony Bloom writes of a man whom he was
privileged to know for many years:

During the war he was arrested and sent to a concentration

camp. When he came back I asked him, 'What have you brought back? What is left of you?' His answer was, 'I have lost my peace.' It gave me a shock: I expected not the loss of something but the gaining of something. I said, 'Do you mean that you lost your faith?' He said, 'No, but I have come back with anguish in my heart.' . . . While a prisoner in the concentration camp, submitted to all the hard and cruel conditions of the camp, suffering continually from the brutality of the system, step by step, hour by hour, meeting after meeting, in pain and anguish, he could yet say, 'Lord forgive; they do not know what they do.' He could, from early morning to the moment he went to sleep, forgive every act of injustice and cruelty he had to endure. He said, 'While it was so, I felt I could intercede before God for the salvation of these men, because at every moment my words were, "I forgive, Lord, forgive them because they do not know what they are doing!" These words, supported by the evidence of actual suffering, gave me a right to ask God for their forgiveness.'[9]

Most of us would not have the largeness of heart of that man, but one weekend, by a chance encounter, one of the writers met the uncle of a young eighteen-year-old girl who had been recently murdered. He talked of the prayer his mother, Isobel's grandmother, had written when she had been in the depths of grief one night over her granddaughter's death. Later the grandmother wrote about the prayer in a letter: 'Murder is so ugly and I wanted to counteract it with something beautiful and also I wanted to try to help her young friends who were devastated . . . If my prayer can help anyone who goes through such an experience I am only grateful.' The prayer ends,

> We pray, O Lord,
> for the poor sick boy
> who caused her sudden death.
> May he one day know your forgiveness.[10]

Jean Vanier's book *The Broken Body* has three parts; in the third part, 'Restoring the Broken Body to Wholeness', he writes:

Forgiveness is the acceptance of our own brokenness,
yours and mine.

Forgiveness is letting go of unrealistic expectations of others
and of the desire that they be other than they are.

Forgiveness is liberating others to be themselves,
not making them feel guilty for what may have been.

Forgiveness is to help people flower, bear fruit,
and discover their own beauty.[11]

Perhaps we have to start with ourselves. Forgiveness itself is
a grace; it requires our hard work and co-operation. Do not
underestimate the difficulty. Perhaps one of the most difficult
aspects is to forgive ourselves for forgiving. It makes the whole
earth quake.

POSTSCRIPT: On forgiveness

Forgiveness is warmth. Melting love.
But I am hurt.
My whole self is forged into defence.
I have been wronged. I hurt.
I am barbed. I am cold.

Christians are supposed to be prepared – programmed, you
might say – to forgive. Jesus forgave. He told his disciples to
do so. We are taught to pray for forgiveness too.

But I am a mass of pricking anger. And fear. I do not know
how Christ summoned love from the inmost sanctuary of his
soul. How did he forgive those who were perpetrating unspeakable torture on him? How can a man who is being deliberately
and unjustly killed, because of trumped-up false charges, find
the courage to forgive? How did he find the courage to do what

he told his followers – and us – to do: to forgive those who despitefully use us?

I hurt. How can I possibly forgive them? They are the ones who are truly in the wrong. They have not understood me. They have no idea of the damage they have done, no idea of the havoc they have caused in my life. It is totally unjust. Those who have wronged me are walking free. They are blind to my rawness and pain – completely insensitive to me – crassly ignorant of how it feels from my angle.

A curious thing about Christ is that he did not die in the glow of a martyr's death, because he had no Christian perspective. Did he wonder if it was all a mistake, in his final exhaustion? It must have been an agonizing slow execution. A few women stood around. They were mute. His dearest friends fled from him, unable to offer either love or support. They were caught up in the menacing confusion. Was the struggle to love, to the end, all for nothing?

When I am with friends, my bitter damaged feelings subside. I remember how to laugh. But as soon as I see any of the others who offended me, the coldness avalanches over me; it obliterates all my warmth. I feel as if my heart is stone, yet it is they who are hard-hearted.

Perhaps if they would back down . . . but they are rigid. If I did forgive them it would do no good. They would still be stiff, while I am a turmoil of bitterness and resentment. If I forgive them, I should be letting myself down. I should have to forgive myself for not having the guts to stick to my own side. How could I bear to see myself in that sort of light? Soft. Weak. I should have to let go of the picture that I have of myself and then where should I be? A fluid, fluctuating person is no use to anyone. I should be at the mercy of every current in the stream, blown by every eddy of the wind. There would be no strength in me.

Weak. Soft. It makes me wonder how Christ found the courage to forgive?

It takes courage to let go: incredible courage to relinquish life in the way he did. That night in the Garden, he sweated blood in his agony. His integrity to love is beyond me. He was exposed in a way I cannot comprehend. He felt all the unbending, flinty hardness of people's hearts. His humiliation was extreme. He had to let go of everything.

> Can I dare to let my stoniness begin to melt?
> Have I got the courage to let go?
> Have I the courage to forgive?

7

FUNERALS

What is man that thou art so mindful of him?
Thou hast made him a little lower than the angels and
crowned him with glory and honour.

Dust thou art and unto dust shalt thou return.

Humankind has wrestled with what happens at death and after,
ever since the first Stone Age man rocked on his heels beside
the corpse of his wife. What did he think had happened to her?
Where now was the life that had been within her? What did the
rest of the tribe do for him? And for the corpse? At what stage
did *homo sapiens* develop reverential disposal of the dead, as
opposed to leaving the remains for the elements and the birds
and beasts of prey to consume?

Such questions have the power to leave us all at sea, so we
seek the hoped for terra firma of contemporary understanding;
some of this has been supplied by Peter Berger, a sociologist
of religion. He points out that every society tries to make
sense of the whole of life, even the painful aspects which many
individuals would like to deny. So each society constructs rituals
to mark significant events in life.[1]

In most societies the funeral is an important event, an
occasion paradoxically filled with celebration, the celebration
of the dead person's life and perhaps achievements, besides grief
and sadness at the death and a recognition of our mortality. It
is a rite of passage. It is a method of ritualizing and acknowledg-

ing grief corporately. Funeral rites throughout the ages have reflected both the customs and beliefs of the people, though we often have difficulty in establishing what the beliefs are. People feel that they want to 'do the right thing' for their relatives (just like weddings) and they settle for the conventional service on offer, advertisements in the paper, the local priest or a duty clergyperson at the cemetery or crematorium, a time slot of half an hour (what that may contain is not always either clear or revealed until it happens), and a family gathering afterwards with its usual social delights and hazards. The predominant pattern in Britain is still that of one of the mainstream Christian denominations. If, for example, you believe that death is the beginning of total oblivion and that the idea of an afterlife is a misconception, you will probably want the funeral director to avoid a Christian service, but if you are in shock, following the death of someone close, you may not be able to make such a coherent decision.

Obviously, the creative opportunities in this event are enormous and the chances of an inadequate or inappropriate event are commensurately high. Weddings are also major rites of passage and the preparations are often lengthy. But funerals have to be planned quickly and the person most affected by the death often has to make the arrangements. Here, the sensitivity of the officiant can make a great deal of difference. By being as empathic as possible with the mourners, and respecting their belief systems or the lack of them, the officiant can do much to make the ritual personal to the mourners, without abandoning the ground on which he or she stands.

The Leicester Co-operative Funeral Service which deals with about 4,000 funerals per year, more than half of all funerals in Leicestershire, tells me that the number of funerals in which there is no minister is less than one per cent. The absence of an officiating minister probably implies that the deceased had no particular faith allegiance, or was agnostic or atheist.[2] The table on the next page shows the relative numbers of funerals in various faith communities over a period of six months in 1991 directed by the Leicestershire Co-operative Funeral Service.

C of E	RC	METH	BAPTIST	ASIAN	OTHER	TOTAL
1031	119	116	60	85	110	1521
67.8%	7.8%	7.6%	4.0%	5.6%	7.2%	100%

Such is the power of convention that only the intrepid try to change the system. Jane Spottiswoode, whose husband Nigel died in 1987, tells of her struggle to 'funeralize' him in her enthusiastic book *Undertaken with Love*.[3] He was an ardent conservationist who abhorred waste, had no time for religion and whose wishes for his funeral included that there should be no unnecessary expense and that his remains should go on the compost heap. Buying a coffin was the hardest part, but eventually one was found.

In the same year, Jane was invited by BBC Radio 4 to make a programme about her DIY experience, which led to considerable publicity as well as responses which highlighted the central responsibility of the ministers and funeral directors for the creation of a helpful event. Indeed, her book with its iconoclastic tone may even achieve what the prophets are always after – fair dealing and honesty – though flat-pack coffin kits may take some time to catch on! The resistance of the funeral industry to her needs and wishes apparently without reasonable grounds was remarkable. It may be that the churches will be encouraged to adapt to people's wishes to create an event which reflects the belief (or absence thereof) of the deceased, while not abandoning the Christian content. Or perhaps it will be necessary for funeral directors to introduce the opportunities suggested by the British Humanist Association and the National Secular Society.

But priests and ministers are responsive to bereaved people's desires at this most sensitive of times. As the officiant, it seems to me that the ritual of the funeral service and the address are both equally important. The ritual is the framework which the mourners can use to plan a service which will reflect perhaps the views and certainly the individuality of the deceased; and the address is a central personal point which can evoke his or her uniqueness. I usually begin funerals by focusing my own mind on what we are trying to do by saying (with variations):

We have three things to do in this service: the first is to give thanks for N. and all that s/he meant to us. The second is to commend N.'s soul into the hands of her/his Creator. (Sometimes I expand here to recognize the difficulties this concept may hold for the unbeliever, agnostic or atheist.) The third task is to pray for one another as we all grapple with the enormity of death.

I attended the potentially very sad funeral of stage and television writer A. B. Only fifty years old, he had collapsed and died while out walking, and left a wife and two talented daughters of eleven and thirteen. The funeral service (Anglican) had been carefully composed by his wife and the parish priest, and as it unfolded with hymns, reading, silences, music on tape and an address, so the unique character and personality of A. B. was evoked.

The address was not a eulogy: it was honest about the dead man's abrasiveness. It was a celebration of a life: it was a thanksgiving. And because it was honest it brought to the fore the man's infectious sense of fun. It was a happy–sad funeral: perhaps the best kind.

A similarly appropriate event was requested by the widow of a Latin-American refugee. Again the death was tragic and premature. He had gone to work for the early shift, hit a patch of black ice and struck a lamppost. The hospital did what they could for the brain haemorrhage, but he never emerged from the coma and he died two years later. The refugee community and friends where he and his family lived at the time attended the crematorium chapel in force to support the young widow and her children. A guitarist played the haunting melodies of Chilean freedom songs before the service began; a fellow refugee spoke movingly, and in English for the benefit of the whole congregation, about the deceased's contribution to the struggle for freedom in his oppressed country. It was an extremely moving event, both for the participants and for me, the officiant. I used the conventional C. of E. Service (ASB) and I felt I had facilitated an event which was as far as possible congruent both to me and to the participants, with their amalgam of political and religious beliefs. I had shared with people, many of whom I knew reasonably well, in acknowledging the transition, in feeling the necessary feelings of grief, sadness and respect. This was in contrast to many funerals where the feelings are either quashed or forbidden, and where the impression is given that the event is a necessary evil and to be dealt with as quickly as possible. If I have to officiate at such a funeral, afterwards I feel drained and exhausted, and in some sense cheated of my proper role. I often have a sense of life denied, even – and this is most tragic – a sense of unlived life. Such a funeral cannot, as A. B.'s and this refugee's did, support the participants and strengthen their faith.

Funerals like these two may have gone some of the way to satisfy the ideals of Julian Litten, the most recent chronicler of the history of funerals, who says in the introduction to his beautifully illustrated book:

> It is my earnest wish that a re-evaluation of the English funeral takes place soon, incorporating the best of the past and the best – if there is any – of today; there, conjoined, refined and purified, we may well have a ritual which suitably expresses those caring and loving attributes so jealously guarded in the past which now seem, sadly, to be dormant in the nation's soul.[4]

I share his wish, but I suspect that liberal-minded people may also want funerals to reflect the pluriformity of our society and its varying beliefs.

The Church of England's Liturgical Commission gave a five-fold answer to the question, 'What should we be doing at a funeral service?':

1. To secure the reverent disposal of the corpse.
2. To commend the deceased to the care of our heavenly Father.
3. To proclaim the glory of our risen life in Christ here and hereafter.
4. To remind us of the awful certainty of our own coming death and judgement.
5. To make plain the eternal unity of Christian people, living and departed, in the risen and ascended Christ.

There may be widespread questioning of these objectives, which would be healthy. But I think it is possible that they may be achieved through the use of several forms,[5] depending on the family's wishes. I shall only consider the funeral service in the Alternative Service Book (ASB), which is clear and succinct without loss of dignity. In fact it allows a *gravitas* which is obscured in the 'old service',[6] despite its dignified and beautiful prose. The ASB service also encourages a proper emphasis on the ritual aspect of a funeral by its conclusion of the service in church with the prayer of commendation:

> Heavenly Father, by your mighty power you gave us life, and in your love you have given us new life in Christ Jesus. We entrust *N* to your merciful keeping, in the faith of Jesus Christ.

Perhaps this is part of the best of the past Litten wishes for, and he describes more in his account as follows,

> In the early Church death was regarded as a release from the trials and tribulations of a wicked and sinful world to a larger, fuller life in heaven . . . death was the last stage of the weary pilgrimage, heaven the goal, Christ the prize. There was good reason, then, for the funeral to be a joyful event, though it would be erroneous to say that it lacked solemnity, for the soul of the good and faithful servant had detached itself from the body for a glorious reunion with God. An especial grace was imparted to the family of the deceased were they to invite the poor and needy to share in the funeral feast which follows the burial. This feast was itself an anticipation of the Common Meal to be enjoyed by all in the New Jerusalem when Christ, the Sacrificial Lamb, will invite all to sit at the same board and partake. Such being the case, how could death be regarded with terror, when life was merely being changed, rather than taken away? . . .
>
> Was it not, then, that the funeral was seen both as a celebration to mark the soul's triumphant translation into Paradise and as a means of comfort and reassurance for the bereaved?[7]

Many of these features assuredly still remain, though development has naturally taken place. In particular, the sacred feast became in the course of time the Requiem Mass, which fulfils the functions required of it by Augustinian theology. Augustine's view of the afterlife included purgatory, 'whereby the faithful might be called after death to pass through a purifying fire, before finally receiving the Crown of Life'. In the church in which I was brought up there were many of these ideas which Litton mentions. But the problems with these views in today's intellectual and philosophical climate are unfortunately manifold:

- The world today is hardly regarded, as the early church regarded it, as wicked and sinful, although the concepts of hell and damnation as desirable correctives have recently received publicity.[8] Most orthodox theologians do not consider a conception of the world as sinful and corrupt as a full picture of reality. A creation-centred theology would begin from a different perspective, affirming the essential goodness of all creation.[9] With a more balanced theological picture of life, we will be less than happy to thank God for 'delivering N from the miseries of this sinful world' – a prayer which has been dropped from modern liturgies.

- The churches today are called upon to minister among many with vestigial Christian convictions and a pluriformity of views, which officiants at funerals must respect, even if agreement is not required. My evangelical clergy friends, for example, do not refuse to take the funerals of Freemasons, although they consider Freemasonry to be largely incompatible with Christianity.

- Our contemporary world lacks a metaphysic which provides us with an adequate 'map' of the afterlife, though the poetic vision of John Henry Newman, reinforced by the music of Edward Elgar, creates a persuasive picture which any responsive soul will find difficult to abandon totally.[10] Yet, the concept of purgatory takes its strength from two important basic Christian understandings: first, that God is pure Love, and second that God is a God of forgiveness. The elaborate metaphysical construct of purgatory may help the Christian seeker to penetrate the mystery of God's reconciling love, or it may repel him or her.

- If purgatory requires, for its scenario to be complete, the demons clamouring to take the miscreants and the 'low-born clods of brute earth' (Newman) off to hell, then I am only willing to suspend my disbelief for the duration of Elgar's *Dream*. Yet my twentieth-century theological arrogance treats with scant respect the noble thought of Dante, not to mention Augustine or Aquinas on whom Dante's thought rests. Yet again, purgatory as a Christian teaching is much misunderstood, as Dorothy Sayers points out in her introduction to her translation of Dante's *Divine Comedy:* 'Purgatory is *not* a place of probation . . . All souls admitted to Purgatory are bound for Heaven sooner or later . . . The soul's choice between God and self, made in the moment of death, is final.'[11]

Such assertions fill me with a sense of inconsistency with the loving purposes of God. I also want to protest, *Who knows?* It seems a contradiction, if God, who is almighty, cannot bring his purposes for the salvation of humankind to final fruition. We know that he voluntarily sets aside his power to accommodate the gift of freewill to his creatures, but we have repeated assurances, as in the Epistle to the Hebrews that 'God had provided something better so that they (the witnesses and martyrs of faith) would not, *apart from us*, be made perfect.'[12]

A similar view (known as 'universalism') is held by many of the mystics, such as Julian of Norwich as she endeavoured to make sense of the revelation given to her that,

> All shall be well, and all shall be well,
> and all manner of thing shall be well.[13]

111

Much attention has been given to wrestling with Mother Julian's assertion in the face of the reality of sin and death, and the teaching of the church about hell, for Julian was a devout daughter of the church. Both Richard Harries and Robert Llewelyn write of the difficulties,[14] and I agree with the former, that,

> What now seems irreconcilable, divine love and the Church's teaching on hell, will form part of a larger, graspable pattern.
>
> There is 'yet the great deed that our Lord shall do, in which he shall save his word in all things – he shall make well all that is not well'. She cannot affirm that 'all that is not well' includes hell. But she arouses in us the hope that it can.[15]

It seems to me essential to offer some such ground for the hope that is in us when facing the fact of death, and when confronting the struggle of preparing for, going to, and recovering from a funeral. It is considered fanciful by many people to think of heaven as anything other than 'pie in the sky when I die', of a 'vague state of bliss'. But I want to take seriously the old monk who gave me many hours of attention at Quarr Abbey, and who on one occasion happily admitted, 'Oh, yes, I meditate regularly on the joys of heaven', and promptly found me O *Quanta Qualia* (O what their joy and their glory must be), Peter Abelard's famous hymn.[16] Who knows, moreover, what is the effect of regular meditation on the last two of the five Glorious Mysteries of the rosary, namely, the Assumption of the Blessed Virgin Mary into Heaven and the Crowning of Our Lady as Queen of Heaven amid the joy of the saints of glory? All I can say is that, notwithstanding the fact that I am an heir to the sceptical *Weltanschauung* which prevails today, I am aware that the quality of my perception of humankind and God is subtly changed and enhanced as I meditate on these mysteries. The heights are higher, the depths are deeper, and the creative love of God seems just that much more awesome.

It is the love of God to which I find myself struggling to give expression at the 'really difficult' funerals. At one, when I was still an inexperienced priest, a family member asked me to conduct a service for the daughter of a close friend who had died in childbirth. I felt confused and anxious: why me? What could I say? Fortunately a long train journey gave me time to think, and I decided to tackle the difficulties head on. With youthful optimism, I spoke of three temptations that often come: the temptation to break down, give way and escape, to find refuge in tears. At first this is a healthy release, but it needs discipline for the sake of others for whom we have responsibility. This may have helped the mother of the girl, perhaps not the father. I would give more value to tears now (see chapter 8). Then there is the temptation to harden one's heart; to build a protective wall around oneself; not to risk loving again, so that one will not be hurt. Maybe this cannot be controlled by the self, but its dangers should not be overlooked. The third temptation perhaps is to lose faith or to twist it. At its simplest there is the common argument that runs, 'If God exists and is almighty, if He is Love, then He wouldn't have allowed this to happen.' It is probably foolish at a funeral to enter this kind of debate, because the remark is probably a protest rather than the opening gambit in a theological conversation. On this occasion I suggested that in the creation of humankind, God limited himself to certain natural rules. Or if this were a protest, and the consequence might be that the protester was going to abandon his or her faith, then it would seem rather foolish to throw away the resources of the wisdom and insight of the faith when you most need it. (We have already seen John Taylor's moving contribution to this theme in chapter 6, page 97.)

This wisdom would include the perception that God seems to be most deeply known in suffering, that Christ is most clearly identified with God when he enters his Father's world and undergoes its pain. This is what I tried to express at the funeral of G., a twenty-five-year-old victim of salmonella poisoning with a daughter aged three. I found myself compelled to say:

> I am not here to give false comfort, or to cry peace where there is no peace . . . I am here . . . to help you face the tragedy of her loss at so young an age. We can face this with courage or fortitude – if we are strong, and some are

stronger than others. But what of faith, when Jesus himself could cry, 'My God, why hast thou forsaken me?'? Faith is not blind acceptance, as in 'It is God's will' – it is clearly *not* God's will that G. should have died, or hospital staff and surgeons would not have worked so hard to save her life. It is God's will that we should have life and have it more abundantly.

It is part of the mystery of suffering that G. was destroyed by a rare strain of salmonella; and it is part of our faith as Christian people that we should trustingly enter that mystery of suffering, with the companionship of Christ, and work it through. We know we shall feel hurt, anger, despair; but we shall (I hope) come back to trusting God that we can endure and emerge with a greater love than before, a love which will enable us to value human life more, a love which will enable us to serve God better – it may even be that that Love will encourage us to take Environmental Health more seriously as a result of our involvement in this tragedy.

I know very little more of the effect of this event on the lives of the participants, except that the hurt young widower found a hurt single mother with a similarly aged child who got on famously with his daughter. I was honoured to perform the marriage ceremony some years ago. But the possibility of the failure of my words to meet the reality of the suffering of the bereaved still has the power to unsettle me.

When it is appropriate, I sometimes fall back on a pattern for a funeral address which I heard from my first vicar, Len Tyler, when I was a curate thirty years ago. It is a useful pattern because it starts from the realities and fears of contemporary humankind.

FEAR	THEOLOGICAL RESPONSE
of separation	the Communion of Saints
of judgement (heaven and hell)	the forgiveness of sins
of meaninglessness	the resurrection and eternal life

It allows us to weave patterns of meaning around the experience of the deceased and his or her friends and relatives, so that the essential hope of Christian faith engages accurately and appropriately with the recollections of the reality of the deceased's life and aspirations. But it is still a tremendous struggle to clothe the ideas in words which will communicate some realistic truth. It is not a hopeless task, but it sometimes feels an almost impossible one.

The further problem arises: what happens to this convenient scheme of things when you are faced with apparent nothingness? What happens when you are faced with either inarticulacy amongst the relatives of the deceased, or a dull despair, or a dreadful sense of what Jung called 'the unlived life'? What happens when you attend a funeral of a very old recluse, or a person who has been locked in upon himself for as long as anyone can remember?

Just because it is easier to weave patterns of meaning around those whose lives have been rich, it does not mean in those cases where life has not apparently been fulfilled, that the Christian verities, which have been hammered out under almost all imaginable conditions of life, become somehow inapplicable. They may be stretched; they may become in certain situations unbelievable. But they do not become the less *true*. So, when one of the Night Shelter workers (see also chapter 5) took it upon herself to arrange the funeral of one of the residents, her godly love stimulated her ingenuity to present a moving and wholesome event, which was appropriate and respectful, where the conventional 'C. of E.' service could have been a hollow sham. There was much silence, a poem another resident had written, and recorded music. We had precious time to reflect on the man's character, which was rich despite being often deeply hidden behind the protective wall of violence and self-destructiveness expressed in his alcohol addiction and argumentativeness. Who knows whether it was a *Christian* funeral or not? Christians were present and were praying silently. 'Thou knowest, O Lord, the secrets of our hearts.'[17]

If funerals are for the living rather than for the dead, then this one was appropriate, just as the elaborate requiem in Norwich Cathedral was appropriate for Frank whose life is celebrated in chapter 3. This took the form of a fully celebrated high mass, with incense, black vestments, the singing of the *Dies Irae* and the Russian *Kontakion for the Departed*, and a splendid eulogy by the Dean of St Paul's. It was followed by a cross-country ride to the medieval churchyard at Brampton, a further speech by the local rector in the biting wind, and finally interment.

Another service specially written and compiled for the occasion was equally elaborate, but consisted of parts of the Anglican Alternative Service Book service with selected readings from Dag Hammarskjöld's *Markings*, Isaiah (40:18–31), the hymn 'Lord of all hopefulness', silences and some striking prayers composed by Jim Cotter. Also printed on the service paper were passages for silent meditation, one of which I include as a witness to the spiritual resources and courage of the bereaved parents, who at the time thought they had lost their son through suicide. It was not until six weeks later that the coroner's report arrived with details of the rare illness which killed him.

> Drink deep of the chalice of grief and sorrow, held out to you by your dark angel of Gethsemane: the angel is not your enemy, the drink, though sharp, is nourishing, by which you may come to a deeper peace than if you pass it by, a 'health of opened heart'.[18]

Did those parents, like Mary, eventually benefit from the sword that pierced their hearts also?

I approach all funerals with a mixture of apprehension and satisfaction: apprehension, for fear of engagement in the struggle with people as they take the first steps in facing the death usually of someone close, with the emotional depths to be plumbed; satisfaction, because I enjoy helping people work with their feelings and often we all grow through this deep experience.

One of the privileges of being asked to take a funeral service is being allowed to see glimpses of the whole person, far beyond the immediate present. Most funerals are for people who have lived for several decades, and as the relatives talk about the person they have known, I become aware of so much more than the tired or ill person I have been visiting – someone who has revelled in dancing, or campaigned for the underprivileged, someone who in their younger days was a great traveller, or who was one of the first to broadcast about ecology. The funeral rites are the last service the relatives can offer to this person in his or her mortal form and it is of great importance to pay tribute to the essentially unique nature of the deceased, and the discussions at this time are often profound and revealing.

Bill was a brilliant and gentle man who died of cancer in his seventies, after two or more years of various treatments, supported by his strikingly determined and capable wife. I saw Bill becoming weaker and weaker. My monthly visits with the Blessed Sacrament were interpolated by more frequent visits. At the end of each visit I always gave him a brief informal benediction. During one visit, I was so struck by his accepting and serene demeanour, that I felt prompted to say 'You know, Bill, though I am giving you a blessing, when I leave, I often feel it is you who are giving me a blessing.' Thereafter, at the end of every visit, until he could no longer speak, he said 'God bless you, David', and I felt profoundly honoured.

His funeral was planned in the best possible way, with the whole family: his wife, his son and daughters and their partners and even a very young grandson, making suggestions, modifying their views, sharing perceptions, remembering, talking about the dead man, pausing to weep, comforting each other. I remember leaving this encounter and shedding my own tears of loss and relief as I drove away.

As an event, a funeral can be an ordeal with the chief mourners 'on show', and it is frequently necessary for the officiant to give permission to release feelings. There was sacred space at this funeral: Bill's life was celebrated, his soul commended to God, and, dare I say, the glory of the risen Christ in him was glimpsed; and I sensed that the work by his family of accepting the pain of his loss was begun.

POSTSCRIPT: The near-death-experience

Will it help me to face death better if I know what is going to happen to me? Recent research into near-death-experiences

(NDEs) suggests that it could. There is a growing body of material collected mainly in America which provides many corroborating accounts of a common experience of people who have clinically died and returned. It began with the discoveries of Raymond Moody,[19] continued by Dr John Sabom,[20] that a number of people who had either suffered heart attacks or severe wounds in war (mostly in Vietnam) gave astonishingly similar versions of what happened to them. Here is a typical story:

> I was in excruciating pain. The doctor was pounding my chest, when suddenly all the pain ceased and I was looking down from a corner of the ceiling of the ward at the doctor and nurse bent over me. My wife was weeping, and I felt sorry for her but at the same time detached. Next, I seemed to fly into a dark tunnel at a great speed, and I said to myself, 'I really ought to go back'. But on I flew until I saw a light, a beautiful light such as I have never seen before, a welcoming light. When I came into the light, I saw figures beckoning me, I recognized one. It was my father who had died years ago. He smiled at me, and said, 'You must return, there is much for you to do.' Immediately, I was back in the ward, the doctor was still pounding my chest and I heard them saying, 'He's gone, I think'. The pain was still there but less now. The doctor stopped for breath, and I breathed too.

The common pattern is fourfold: first, out of the body with cessation of pain. The objective reality of this experience is supported by the person observing activity which would otherwise have been out of their line of vision, as, for example, seeing a person in a red pullover walking along a corridor outside the room and only visible through high windows. Second, the person feels that they are moving along a dark tunnel. Third, at the end of the tunnel there is light into which the person emerges and it is an experience filled with wonder and joy. Fourth, other people emerge from the light to meet the subject, who reports, variously, recognizing and being recognized by significant others – departed relatives, friends, Christ or other gurus, depending on religious orientation. At any stage it is possible for the person to return, sometimes only as a result of conversations with the people who are met. The return into the body is also a return to the pain and suffering which was previously felt.

Most of the people who have had this experience speak of a radical change in their lives, attitudes and outlook which it has effected in them. They testify to their loss of the fear of death; they speak of the preciousness of life, of a new valuation they have of relationships and the importance of all that is. They frequently, on recovery, change their work to something which is more worthwhile, as if their brush with mortality had given a clear moral framework previously missing from their lives.

There is an old hymn which runs,

> The heavenly child in stature grows
> And growing learns to die.

I do not know whether the metaphysical map of the afterlife (or at least the beginning of that afterlife) revealed by the evidence of NDE research is scientifically or philosophically acceptable. It must certainly be taken into consideration. What matters is that such experiences actually contribute to our overall approach to death and dying.

We can also benefit from reading *The Last Letter to the Pebble People*[21] because it tells us of the courageous last journey of Aldie Hine as he resolved the unfinished business of his fractured relationships with friends and relatives, and in so doing prepared himself for death. His wife wrote,

> I now know what people mean when they say they feel uncomfortable in the presence of a truly holy man. Death makes all men briefly holy, if we let it. Such a look wipes out all pretence. There is nowhere to hide. It simply sweeps away anything that gets in the way of cleansing love . . .
>
> One weeps when one knows one's self to be wholly revealed and wholly accepted for a moment. It is like being forgiven – for nothing, for everything.[22]

He 'managed' his own death with great dignity. His and his family's handling of his anticipated death from cancer is a model of sensitivity, emotional clarity and struggle, of honesty and love. So is the way in which they managed the funeral arrangements and an informal memorial event, at which Aldie's wife spoke so movingly. One aspiration which struck me as being of immense significance was part of Virginia Hine's prayer at the memorial service:

> We recognise that there are forces too powerful for us to handle, which work to separate us from each other and from you (O God). We commit ourselves and those who live here with us into your care for protection from these alienating forces.

A holy and happy death may not be granted to us, but such examples as Aldie Hine, and many another from our personal experience, indicate that we may have some degree of control over our manner of departure. Christians conventionally pray for a holy and happy death. If that becomes an earnest prayer, spilling over into action, then our lives will be transformed, in the same way as many of the lives of those who have experienced near-death have been transformed.

8

PAST LOSS

The randomness of life is a given fact. There is no answer to why I have been born in a green and pleasant land, with a temperate climate and education for all as a norm, while my contemporaries are precariously eking out their existence in drought-stricken Somalia, or fleeing as refugees from Mozambique, contending with violence in Bosnia Herzogovina, or the Gaza strip. There is no answer to why I am in a situation where I can take myself off to a tiny hermitage from where I can watch the sun shining pinkly through lambs' ears as they crop lush, glittering grass, while others are trapped in drab streets which look out only on to grey pavements, more pinched cramped housing and ugly slab factory buildings.

'God helps those who help themselves.' Maybe. But in the material sense there seems to be only randomness.

Most of the time we live without wonder within the situation in which we find ourselves. Where there is illness, I hear people say 'If there were a God, he wouldn't let this happen', referring to the suffering of their partner, their parent or their child; but there is no inbuilt system of reward for a life well lived, nor punishment for viciousness and cruelty. Perhaps you know the infinitely tender recitative in the setting of the St Matthew Passion by J. S. Bach for the words, 'Er hat uns allen wohl gethan' – 'To all men Jesus good hath done'. And yet this man was executed. If there were just deserts for living a godly life, then this human being of all human beings might have been protected from such a fate.

Striving to make sense of life or working to create order out of chaos is a way of keeping anxiety at bay, but as Rabbi Harold

Kushner shows in his book *When bad things happen to good people*,[1] if we dare to examine the evidence around us, so-called good people are no more safe from physical harm than so-called bad people – 'so-called', because no one is entirely one or the other. It is not as simple as the goodies and the baddies in the cowboy films, something Job discovered centuries before Christ.

In a play by Archibald Macleish, the wife of the main character says to her husband, 'Cry for justice and the stars will stare until your eyes sting. Weep, enormous winds will thrash the water. Cry in sleep for your lost children, snow will fall.'[2] There is no justice in the randomness of life.

The experience of being bereaved of someone very dearly loved is a time of crisis when the feeling of chaos threatens to break every strand of life. The gaping wound is so shocking and so huge that for some people healing seems beyond possibility. One of the most painful aspects of bereavement that adds to the chaos of the internal earthquakes is that the feeling of loss reawakens all the other losses that have ever been experienced. Grief resonates with all other griefs: it reverberates with all the emptiness and loneliness that have ever been lived through. We are brought face to face with the inevitability and the finality of death – whatever our beliefs in an afterlife – and with our ultimate aloneness. Our response to the shattering nature of the crisis may be to hide and to sink because the pain is too great, and the world is too chaotic in its meaninglessness; or it may be to crawl out from the wreckage and accept the possibility of redemption, healing, hope and love.

In the same way that Frank felt we on the outside had no right to say the persecuted should offer forgiveness to the persecutor (see chapter 6), I do not feel I have any right to try to influence the choices of a person suffering the anguish of grief after the death of a deeply loved one. Each one has his or her own response, whether it is to turn to the wall and close off from life or whether it is to gather up resources and find from within an affirmation of life. For each person there are decisions about hope and despair, and thus about life and death. Neville Ward writes:

It is probable that we fear the world within as much as the world without, especially the accumulations of dismay and anger deposited in our lives as life has flowed by uncaught, unused, carrying so much out of sight. Some of this emotion relates to genuine injury and injustice we have been unable to forgive, some belongs to our earliest experiences of insecurity in childhood . . . We carry around a self that could, we fear, get the better of us one day.[3]

At the time of bereavement, the pain of tearing away all that was normal and comforting and ordinary reveals starkly all the other pain. A child, weeping inconsolably after his small black mongrel puppy had died, was weeping not only for the pain of losing the warm, vital, furry little creature, but for the reminders of the pain of being lonely, of being himself an outsider; his tears were the hot bitter tears of rejection.

There are, however, times when people seek help, and it seems that even when they have been unable to overcome their grief, the very act of asking for help is a stirring of the sense that there may be some way of pulling themselves out of the quicksands that are sucking them under.

During our lives each of us is touched by various people and events. These are significant to us in some particular way, whether for good or ill. There are parents of course with their 'good enough'[4] – or otherwise – nurturing, and there may be siblings with the inevitable and concomitant jealousies, rivalries and companionship. There are other relatives, who may have introduced or awoken in us joy in music, or nature, or sport, or who may have intruded, bringing unwelcome fear. There are our friends, and there are the friends of parents who have to be accommodated when we are children. There are teachers, colleagues and bosses. Each of us has a unique collection of such people in the background, and it seems that sometimes we do not realize how significant any of these people are until the echoes return from the past. We may be aware of the importance of the person, but may not always recognize the relevance of a particular event, until in trying to make sense of the chaos we start again to sift through the accumulations of dismay and anger.

Joan, a middle-aged woman, had been married for some twenty years and her children had left home. Her husband, Peter, had recently negotiated a new career and they had moved into a different part of the country. She found herself feeling unaccountably angry with him and eventually decided to seek help. A friend suggested the local Relate (marriage guidance) office, and with some foreboding and anxiety she made an appointment with a Relate counsellor. It was not long before she revealed the fact that the last time she had moved into a new area was many years ago, shortly after her father had died.

> He died very quickly. It was awful really. He hadn't long remarried. The Doctor had thought his pains were arthritis; it wasn't until I insisted he went for a second opinion that they found he had cancer. I felt angry with everybody. But you have to get on with things, don't you? And we had to move for Peter's work. And the children were little.

It seemed there had not been any time for her to grieve properly for her father, nor to reflect on her feelings about the move, because of family pressure. This disclosure was, however, only part of the way back to the beginning of her silted-up griefs.

In this recent move, she had left the house where all the children had been brought up, so losing a place of memories with many roots, and the disturbance of moving had not been just the upheaval of the practical arrangements. In the parallel move after her father's death, she had left the area in which she and her parents had always lived, and her father's death had come at the end of a sequence of events which had left Joan feeling sore, very hurt and misunderstood.

When she was twelve, her parents had decided to separate after years of acrimony, and Joan had stayed with her father and older brother and sister. She had felt angry with her mother for the way she had treated her father, and she was glad her mother was no longer living under the same roof with them. Her father was somewhat anxious after the marriage break-down, and the family decided to buy a dog so that Joan was not alone in the house for too long before her brother and sister returned from school and her father came back from work. Joan was delighted with the dog and did her best to train him herself. He was called Kim. He was not entirely a model of virtue, in spite of Joan's efforts, as he had a very individual streak in him, but he was a well-loved friend.

Joan had left Kim with her father when she had gained a place at a teacher training college, and it had seemed natural then, as Joan was engaged to be married, to leave him with her father as he was still living alone. Joan's father found a new woman friend. Joan was doubtful about her at first, but seeing her father's happiness, she gradually accepted her. There was, however, a difficulty: the woman had a dog, and her dog and Kim had taken instant and fur-flying dislike to each other. Kim was now twelve years old, but he was by no means decrepit, and his individuality was not diminished. Joan pondered and worried. Her father would not say anything to her about Kim being a nuisance, but it was clear that Kim was the biggest obstacle in the way of him setting up home with his new woman friend. Eventually, when Joan was staying at her father's home at Christmas, with her husband and two small twins, she took the only way out she could think of: having fed the babies and left Peter in charge, she collected the lead and the dog, took him out for a last walk, and then to the local vet to have him put down.

She walked alone for as long a time as she could before returning, working hard to regain control of her emotions. When she turned the key in the front door, she was plunged again into the domestic chores. She succeeded in keeping up a brave front, and no one, not her husband who was not a dog lover, nor her father, realized what she had put herself through. She buried her grief in the washing of nappies, comforting herself as best she could by keeping busy.

Her father remarried, but in less than a year he had died and a few months later, she and Peter had moved to Sussex.

Only now that she had come for help was she able to mourn the loss of her home, the loss of her father, the loss of her parents' marriage, the loss of her mother through the divorce and the loss of Kim. It was only now that she was able to understand that her anger with Peter was connected with her anger with her father, who had died so soon after Joan had carried out the terrible decision to have Kim put down, a decision which had made her feel like a murderer. And it was only when she recognized her anger with her father that she saw a glimpse of what lay behind her parents' decision to separate, and she began to mourn the loss of her mother through that separation. In this recent move, when she and Peter had left their home in Sussex, she had felt lonely and shut off from him, unable to communicate with him; he had felt frustrated with her in her greyness and had been unable to reach her.

So many events and so many powerful and unwelcome emotions were tangled up for her in the apparently simple practical step of relocating herself in a new area, that it was several months of hard, painful struggle before she could face with equanimity herself with her griefs, her husband who had occasioned the move, and her home with its new possibilities.

John Wren-Lewis writes:

> The root of human alienation lies in personal life itself – at the most intimate level, where each person faces (or avoids facing) his own inner life, and is involved in relationships with other individuals, on the basis of recognizing them (or directly refusing to recognize them) as beings with the same kind of inner life. [5]

Daring to face the secrets of the inner life takes a great deal of courage. Joan's recognizing of herself, with her own mixture of passionate love and bitter resentment, was what she began to explore after the move from Sussex. She began to see herself and Peter and each of her parents as ordinary, fallible human beings. For Joan it was not the bereavement of a person that reawakened buried losses, it was the other way round: the loss of her home in the present time brought to the surface all the unmourned bereavements of the past.

In the Chinese language, the same word is used for both 'crisis' and 'opportunity', and it seems that for Joan the crisis of moving house offered her the necessary opportunity of daring to face her inner world, so that she and Peter could begin again on a better footing in their marriage. This time of crisis which can offer opportunity reveals that although outward circumstances may be random, there is some kind of inner wisdom, which, when allowed to unfold, can bring healing or reconciliation to the inner world, so that the journey can continue less impeded by the weight of past losses.

A child psychologist, talking to a group of parents with adopted children, was explaining how adolescence is a time of trying to establish the newly burgeoning self, of searching for the background that makes sense of developing traits. It may be a particularly difficult time for adopted children of course, where there are so many unknowns. Parents normally watch out for squalls as puberty looms up; the children put in growing spurts, demand licence for various hair-raising exploits, expect greater freedom, and generally test the strength of the boundaries of both parental control and trust. The psychologist explained that teenagers are trying, amongst other things, to get right all the things that were not properly sorted out the first time round – during that first turbulent testing in the pre-school years when they were no longer infants, safely strapped into high chairs and baby buggies, but were exploring to the length and breadth of their abilities (and their parents' tolerance!). For adopted adolescents whose beginnings were interrupted, and whose family roots may be unknown, the exploring of the expanding world may be more than usually enticing or threatening. For children whose parents have died, there are similar difficulties. Nevertheless, these teenage years are certainly a time of opportunity which has to be grabbed as it may never occur again, and the moment for strengthening the bond between child and parents, whether natural or adopted, may be missed.

Two members of the group that the psychologist was addressing were the father and mother of three adopted children, two girls and a boy. Recently these parents had opened the door to a police officer; their feelings had turned to consternation and dread as he told them the reason for his visit: the two elder children had been caught shoplifting. The parents felt they had completely failed their girls; they had sensed the irritability and unrest in the air, but had not expected delinquency. A probation officer had come to visit them to make reports and to talk to the two teenage girls, aged thirteen and fifteen. The police did not proceed with charges, but some hard talking was obviously necessary.

127

Both girls had felt resentful when the mother of the family had gone to Wales, because her elderly father had suffered a severe stroke. After his death, which was in many ways a relief, she returned home to find the thirteen-year-old defiant and scornful, and her unruly behaviour then escalated to this episode of shoplifting. In the talk around the table that followed, the mother realized that this middle daughter was pushing at all the boundaries. As a baby, she had been placed in a nursery and then various foster homes before adoption; now she was testing how much her mother really loved her. Her first mothers had let her go, would this one too?

For the older girl the situation was different: she had always been secretive and withdrawn, and her parents were at a loss to understand her now. They talked with the child psychologist, and told her everything they could think of concerning their elder daughter, who had been somewhat overshadowed by the more flamboyant middle daughter. They knew she had constructed long fantasies for herself about her 'real mum'. The psychologist listened carefully to the parents. After a pause, she said thoughtfully, 'It's a long shot, but I think it might help if she could meet her natural mother.'

The parents were shocked at this. Where did it put them? Were they relegated just to caretakers? Would the other two children want to jump on the band-wagon? Would they lose this daughter if she were to meet her natural mother? They knew she would have the right to search out her mother when she reached the age of eighteen, but now she was only fifteen.

Nevertheless, despite their fears, they decided to do what might be best for their daughter and began a search for her natural mother by contacting the original adoption agency.

After many difficulties in tracing addresses, the natural mother was found and approached. The girl's adoptive parents still had many misgivings, and the mother could not face the meeting with the natural mother. But the father arranged to bring his daughter to the meeting, which was skilfully handled by the adoption worker from the agency. There were many tears and embraces. The natural mother had been overjoyed when contacted by her daughter, whom she had given away for adoption only very reluctantly. The daughter's fantasies about her 'real mum' were now grounded. Strangely enough, she then felt closer to both of her adoptive parents. Her adopted siblings did not at this stage want to follow in her footsteps and initiate searches for their natural mothers. The delinquency of both daughters ceased with the support and encouragement of the adoption worker, the psychologist and the probation officer; the recovery of emotional equilibrium brought the family back on to an even keel, to the profound relief of the parents, and the child psychologist's 'long shot' had paid off. The only sad person in the end was the natural mother who could not replay the events and regain the daughter whom she had lost.

Like adolescence and like Joan's removal to another area, death and bereavement can also offer opportunity for working through earlier difficulties which need resolution for their healing. However, when bereavement has shattered all sense of stability, to face the reverberations it has caused can feel like twisting the knife in a wound which is already causing intolerable pain.

One young man, John, found himself mourning his widowed mother to an excruciating degree and sought help for this part of his journey. His mother had been his only parent since he was three, when his father was killed in a traffic accident. In the course of talking about his relationship with his beloved mother, he began to penetrate the carefully cultivated thickets he had allowed to grow up and hide his childhood memories. He recalled the horror of an event he had buried as of no importance to the present, as it had never been talked of, nor even mentioned since it happened when he was five: he had come into the kitchen and found his mother standing with a glazed, expressionless face, and a sharp kitchen knife in her hand. With the quickness of a child's instant perception, he knew she was about to try to kill herself. He cried out to her and put his arms round her as far as he could reach, and she came to herself. Neither of them had ever spoken about that terrible moment. He had 'forgotten' it until now, twenty-five years later, just over one year after her death.

As he talked, he realized that he had been living for a quarter of a century with the fear of her death, not only because of the tragedy of his father's death, but because he was afraid that if he was not good enough, she would want to commit suicide again. He had dreaded her death, fearing that the world would feel very dangerous without her. It would be intolerable for him. Now the very thing he had most dreaded had happened. In fact, she had died of kidney failure, but it was only in painfully unravelling the trail of events that he allowed himself to believe that he had loved her enough, that it was not through his neglect, nor because he was not good enough, that she had died. He began to recognize that she had in the last years of her life, in spite of her dependence on drugs and hospital treatment, found an inner security which had made suicide an untenable resort. Now that he was able to piece it all together for the first time, talking about it to someone who could understand, he was able gradually to let go of the too-heavy burden of responsibility he had carried since childhood.

John had been very frightened of being left alone in the world, but when he dared to face the frightening truth of the memories he had held secretly locked in the background of all his experiencing, he realized his new freedom in the present. In order to accomplish that, however, he had had to be painfully honest with himself about his relationship with his mother, facing in himself his outraged anger and sense of betrayal that she should ever have considered leaving him.

John felt, as some people do, that although the circumstances of the outer world are largely random, there is some kind of order in the inner world. Although he felt much trepidation in approaching this inner life, he had some intuition or inner wisdom that told him there would be some kind of rationale behind the crisis of his mother's death, which had urged him to continue searching for a way of disarming the threatening chaos.

Death may rob us of the chance to say the last words, of making up the last quarrels, of seeing the familiar person just one more time, of embracing them in one last hug, or it may offer us the chance of inner reconciliation. But the empty space left may remind us of all the other times when the ground has disappeared from in front of us, leaving us on the edge of an abyss. For the elderly man mentioned in chapter 2, the abyss was too frightening to stay near. He felt he could not continue the pilgrimage without his wife. Her death conjured up all the fears of abandonment that he had carried since childhood, and it was too daunting for him to attempt to understand. He refused the help offered him and hoped only that his ulcer would carry him off.

But for others, although in the finality of death relationships cannot be healed in the ordinary sense, there are ways in which wounds may be healed, so that the journey may be continued with less pain.

For forty-year-old Yvonne the death of her mother had caused despair and inner conflict which she was unable to fathom. It was three years since her mother had died, and yet she still felt lost and bewildered, and she still found herself reaching for the phone to ring her mother before she recollected that it was impossible for her mother to answer her call. Her father had died a few years before, but she had not felt so close to him. He had spent many years abroad during her childhood, and to Yvonne he had always seemed rather a stranger who came and went, while her mother was a constant figure.

With a Cruse bereavement counsellor, Yvonne cast around for anything that might throw light on her distress, which had lasted for so long since her mother had died. She remembered a row with her father when she was a teenager, and her mother had gone into hospital for an operation. Her father was jealous of her affectionate relationship with her mother, and shouted at her, 'Your mother isn't all she's made out to be.' She had lashed back at him, that if he were a real man he would make sure that uncle Bob got out of the house and never came back, because uncle Bob, who spent protracted periods with them, was a bully, a man of unpredictable temper and sullen moods, whom she disliked intensely.

As she retold the story of this quarrel, a new slant flashed into her mind. She felt sick as she realized how often uncle Bob had stayed with them in her father's absence, and she fell into a miserable silence. She had known the facts for many years, but had firmly pushed them to the back of her mind, not allowing herself to look at the obvious horrible truth.

She went home and very bravely did some ferreting around

131

in as unobtrusive a fashion as possible about dates and times abroad for her father and when uncle Bob had stayed with them. She came to the appalling conclusion that what she had already guessed, but had not dared to let herself know, was true: she was not her father's child. Her mother had carried on a long drawn-out affair with this man, whose presence she had resented bitterly, and worst of all she was almost certainly his daughter.

Her mother's death had presented her with this crisis; it was a clear opportunity to reshape her inner map of how she saw her family. She had previously experienced herself feeling sorry for her mother, living under uncle Bob's oppressive bullying rule; now she had to absorb the fact that her mother had not only tolerated him, but had enjoyed his attentions, and Yvonne's supposed father had probably taken flight in his trips abroad as a way of escape. She wrestled with the turmoil inside her. She could understand why she had wanted to keep close to her mother with these two alternating men in the household, but she hated the thought of her mother sleeping with uncle Bob, and wondered why her 'father' had put up with this situation.

With all these horrendous thoughts it was a time of acute pain for Yvonne, but gradually she was able to picture her mother as an ordinary frail and vulnerable human being, like herself, and her 'father' as a weak, ineffectual but gentle person, who needed affection as she did. Uncle Bob, she finally realized, must have had some redeeming features for her mother to have found him attractive. She seemed to grow up very suddenly. She was now an adult with her own resources, and though scarred by the experiences she had lived through, she was no longer the little girl (albeit forty years old) wanting to be able to run back to her mum.

> Sticks and stones can break my bones,
> But names can never hurt me.

That is the old adage, but I do not believe it. It had been very painful and hurtful to Yvonne to realize that the abusive label 'bastard' belonged to her. In a much slighter incident, another woman remembered the smarting rejection she had felt as a six-year-old when she overheard her grandmother telling a neighbour how she preferred her grandson to her grand-daughter, because the granddaughter was such a bad-tempered little girl. She never forgot the remark and felt she was always regarded with disfavour. But as a grown-up person, she could place her bad temper in the rightful context of the distress of her anxiety as a child who had been born during the uncertainty of war.

There is a liberating factor in daring to face the truth. Even with all the pain of discovery, like Joan, and the teenage girls and John and Yvonne, we may find that the facts are friendly. These people had needed help from beyond their immediate circle in order to find resolution of their inner turmoil. Their wounds had been too deep for healing without external inter-vention; nevertheless, with courage and patience and the affir-mation of the people they had chosen to trust with their pain, they all found that in fact the truth does set us free.

Not all the past echoes are of such dramatic intensity. An elderly man in mourning for his wife felt overwhelming guilt at his lack of love for her. He had cared for her tenderly in her last illness, and they had spent many hours talking to each other, but after her death he could not eradicate the memory of the quarrel twenty years earlier when she had rejected his sexual advances. Since that time, the only physical affection they had given to each other had been gentle touching when either of them was ill. He knew how much he had missed her physical love, and was filled with remorse at the hardness of heart which had prevented him from approaching her again. He wondered whether she had felt rejected by him. Nothing could be done to alter that now, he could not ask her how she felt about it, nor could he beg for her forgiveness. He spoke with a trusted man friend, in deep embarrassment, and felt his burden lighten as his friend accepted both him and what he was saying without scorn and without judgement. The translated first line of a poem by Prudentius, 'Take him earth for cherish-ing', conveys the tenderness with which this old man wanted to remember his wife.

Most of us, despite the fears that handicap us, and despite

the damage inflicted in the ordinary course of living, can if we look find encouragement from the diversity of fellow pilgrims around us. Most of us lead relatively undramatic lives, but we may be comforted by the Hasidic story of the little man who comes to the gates of heaven. The angelic guard who questions the newly dead postulants asks, 'What brings you to these gates?' The little man replies, 'Truly, Sir, I have no reason to think that you will accept me. I am unworthy, Sir. I am an ordinary and ignorant man.' The angel welcomes him with the words, 'You have gained the realization that you are ordinary and ignorant, and this in itself is a worthy accomplishment. Enter!'

POSTSCRIPT: Reconciliation

Reconciliation is about celebration and about love.

It takes enormous courage to embark on change; without great daring, reconciliation may not be possible at all. It is an immense risk even to change my mind: I may see the other person from a new vantage point, but this will probably involve me in having to scrap my old perception of myself. If I were to look now through new, unscratched lenses, I should have a different outlook. Should I still recognize myself? Do I dare to look in this startlingly clear light? Do I dare to see myself reassembled in a different and altering pattern?

How does the process of reconciliation begin? How does reconciliation between large groups of people take place? When warring groups have their horns locked, neither side has space for different perspectives. At the time of writing, we are on the edge of the Earth Summit meeting in Rio de Janiero; will the climate of acquisition and progressively higher living standards prevail, or will the environmental groups pile the pressure on to the politicians of both the western world and the Third World? President Bush said last month, 'The U.S. cannot afford to put the environment before jobs.' The Third World leaders insist 'that the less developed countries are not about to bow down automatically to the environmental prescriptions of the rich'.[6]

The peace process between the Israelis and the Arabs is in deadlock, as it is between the Armenians and the Azerbaijanis, the Kurds and the Iraqis and the Croatians and the Serbs. Even with peace-keeping forces, mediators and negotiators, the best attempts are wry compromises and hard bargaining. Each side looks at what it must hold to, at great cost, and what it can throw down to try to get a better hand in the end, like a gigantic, very painful and usually tragic game of cards.

Adam Curle writes of the blandishments of those in power. Too often, the reconciliations being brought about by powerful bodies are 'soporifics – amiable words and minor concessions',[7] while underneath the conflicts are still there, deeply rooted and growing.

Is it any different when individual people are at loggerheads with one another? Anxious couples come to the negotiating tables at Relate offices, filled with dreary foreboding about the inevitable compromise and sacrifice they feel they will be compelled to make. When there are the added pressures of time and deadlines, the difficulties are compounded.

One sure characteristic of profound and true reconciliation between individuals is that the process has its own momentum. Although there is a desperate urgency not to hang about, to sort things out before delay makes them worse, to do so in a hurry is usually a false economy of time. It may be that in the slow working out of how they can together find a less tense way of living with one another, they may discover that it is not a case of having to decide what has to be sacrificed – deciding between noisy family life and its companionship perhaps, or peace in a lonely single existence – it may be about having both companionship and peace in the deeper understanding of each other which leads to a better husbanding of resources.

In the gradual changes in working to draw nearer to where we want to be, we may find that whatever were our fears, concerning what we should have to abandon, they are now irrelevant. Whatever baggage has to be thrown overboard on the way seems only incidental compared to the anticipated celebration of arrival.

135

Not the maximum of harmlessness, but the maximum of fruitfulness: together with what may be its unavoidable dangers. That is what we always want.[8]

The maximum of fruitfulness; then there can indeed be celebration. But the unavoidable dangers are very much there. The dangers are often painful, and always require courage to overcome them.

A young couple whose marriage was sailing perilously close to the rocks sought help. She blamed herself for the arguments, feeling very inadequate and helpless, while her husband said he felt rejected. She had left behind her sprightly bounce and independence when she left her job to have two children. Now she felt dull and cabbage-like, a captive to the children, and he was wondering whether to cut his losses and look elsewhere for affection. In the unscrambling of the past from the present they had to face their unmet expectations of each other, and to risk some honest talking about their sense of betrayal. It was many months before they were in full sail again in the open sea; the work had involved the husband daring to persuade his mother to baby-sit, so that they could enjoy each other's company more fully, and the wife putting herself on the line by applying for part-time jobs.

Sometimes the reconciliation experience is not that of the joy of a couple, it is the inner solitary reconciliation of the acceptance that healing can come only through separation. A deep and immensely valuable maturing can take place with the realization that the fault does not lie all at the door of the other, but it may be hurtful and difficult to reach this point. It may be hurtful and humbling to continue to recognize the love that was there in the beginning, while also recognizing that that love has become warped by tension, anger, coldness and disaffection, rendering it impotent to steer through the hazards of the relationship. Only where this responsibility is acknowledged and recognized, with the courage of daring to face whatever this involves, can anything creative follow in the wake of the loss.

Now I wonder about how reconciliation between larger groups can be effected – Muslims and Christians, Sikhs and

Hindus, Catholics and Protestants, trades unions and management. One of the stumbling blocks to reconciliation between individuals is the way each sees the other through prisms of stereotyping, attaching the labels that have become common property instead of using the present situation as a moment with possibilities for responding to the other as the unique individual he or she truly is. Is this what happens in larger groups too?

The terrifyingly urgent task of reconciliation between clashing ideologies, alienating cultures, the rich and the poor, the oppressed and the oppressors hovers over us all.

John Robinson wrote:

> The world indeed does give peace of a kind – at the end of a torpedo; the peace you get by preparing for war. But it is the barren peace of peace-keeping, rather than peace-making, the separating of the combatants rather than bringing them together.[9]

Bringing together the combatants is a daunting but vital element in reconciliation, whether the combatants are the warring elements of the acceptable and unacceptable images within me as an individual, or the two people seeking to reunite after estrangement, or opposing forces dragged to peace talks. It is necessary to keep daring to meet to continue the dialogue. It is necessary to risk our vulnerability and to have the courage to hear the views of the others, because they too, each one, have complex inner reasons for the way they think.

Reconciliation begins with the situation as it is, whatever pain and turmoil and anguish have been incurred, and it continues with the supremely difficult activity of loving. What we most deeply want influences who we are, therefore it is necessary to continue listening while reaching for our own integrity all the time, knowing that we are profoundly responsible for the position we hold, but we do not have the responsibility of changing the attitude of the other.

Love and reconciliation are offered to us by a man who died wretchedly. The task seems wellnigh impossible when this man's life and death are still argued over bitterly. But his death is, paradoxically, celebrated even on this earth in joy.

9

§

THE GIFT OF TEARS

The Lord God drove out the man and sent him forth from the garden of Eden. And Eve was bitter and there was remorse in her soul. In her bitterness as she followed in Adam's footsteps, legend tells us, she bit the top off the last leaf she passed on her way out through the gates, which is why the leaf of the tulip tree has a bite-shaped curve taken from it to this day.

There is another legend that the Lord God, seeing the remorse of Adam and his wife, was moved to pity. He repented of his hardness of heart and he spoke to them thus, My son, Adam, I can see that thou and the woman that I gave thee have great sorrow. There is grief in your hearts for your transgression. In your life henceforth there will be enmity, adversity, and oppression, but I will give you solace. I have determined you shall have a gift more precious than gold. It is this most costly pearl: a tear. When your souls are in pain and tribulation, when you are overcome by your grief, then shall this tear fall from your eyes and you shall be comforted and your burden shall be lightened.

When they heard the Lord God speak thus, Adam and his wife Eve were deeply grieved, and their eyes became fountains of tears which watered the earth. Since that day, the seed of Adam and Eve have wept tears in their pain, and the pain has been eased.

(Old Jewish story)

138

For years I have wondered why I, who always considered that I had a happy childhood and who possess a basically happy disposition, could only remember bad experiences from early childhood. Recently, with a group of friends in whom I felt great confidence, I discovered part of the blight over my childhood innocence.

I retold a story of my experience of the war to them. When I was a child we lived at the top of a hill in the middle of a triangle of airfields which were targets for the German bombers. I was four. My vivid memory replayed a raid one night in 1943, when my father had gone away with the army: I was terrified by the sirens, the explosions, the tiles falling from roofs. And then there was a crack closer than the rest, right outside our house. The window of the downstairs bathroom was shattered and I heard the glass fall into the bath with a crash. My mother left me with my baby sister crying in the Morrison shelter under the grand piano, to go and fetch the Fire Warden a couple of doors down the road. While away, the door must have shut, and when she returned, she called for me to open the door. I remember standing there petrified, two yards from the door, unable to open it, unable to move, speak or cry. As I told the story, I wept – great sobs of horror and fear which I had carried around since those days.

When do we find healing from the past? How can the burdens of the wars which we have all inherited be laid down? As I work with people in counselling I see more and more emotional wounds, sometimes only thinly healed over with vulnerable scar tissue. I am becoming increasingly aware of the legacy of the war, of all wars. For as I know personally, the legacy is reckoned not only in terms of huge loss of life, of limb, of talent, of beauty, of culture, but also loss of mental health and the infliction of disturbance and trauma, especially upon the innocent, which may never be healed.

I have now had fifty-three years of experiencing. In that time, amidst all the deeper events of my life – Confirmation, courtship, childbirth, my ordination, the adoption of two of our children, the death of my father, religious retreats, psychotherapy – I have been conscious of the closeness of joy and tears: together. As I reflect on that truth, the strange phenomenon of my long attraction to and fascination with the music of John Dowland falls into place.

Seemingly by chance, my music teacher at school, Charles Cleall,[1] suggested I try Dowland's 'Now, O now, I needs must part' when I was seventeen. I worked through the other songs in the *First Book of Airs*, revelling in their words and in the fresh spirit of the late Renaissance which they breathed.[2] I only ever sang these songs privately or for a singing lesson. More than twenty years later, when I met a lutenist (David Capp) with considerable gifts of accompaniment, I performed them with The Elizabethans, Sheila Graham's troupe of entertainers. It was then I discovered the immense power of the big melancholy songs of the *Second Book of Airs*. I realized they demanded a total performance, just as German songs are presented at a Lieder Recital. The song then not only 'took me over'; performed thus, it had the power of concentrating the attention of an audience wholly on Dowland's work of art. I was surprised by this power, and felt it most strongly present when singing 'I saw my lady weep'; 'Sorrow, stay'; and 'Flow my tears'.[3] I performed these songs regularly over a period of seven or eight years from the mid-seventies, often wondering at the depth with which they spoke to me.

I began to realize why these songs were so important in 1978. I attended a Person-Centred Approach Workshop for a fortnight at Nottingham University as part of a four-month sabbatical in the midst of an increasingly busy professional life as an industrial chaplain in Norwich. The break came at just the right time, and enabled me to do some inner personal work; and through that, I became aware of a very great sadness within me. I also knew that I had a strong tendency to refuse to acknowledge the sadness which I had been carrying. I suspect that large numbers of people brought up with the emotional controls typical of Britain, and particularly typical of the British male, are unable to acknowledge their deep sadness.

How pervasive is this taboo! Who cannot remember those harsh commands, 'Pull yourself together! Stop blubbing! Control your tears!' And the commands may have been necessary to curtail hysteria or because the disturbance was too great for the rest of the family or group. Contrast this with the knowing parent who cradles the sobbing child and allows the emotion to spend itself. I have been saddened at the vast numbers of people I meet, often at a time of stress and emotion, who say to me 'I haven't cried since I was a child'. Or there was the young widow who said her husband had only cried once, and that was at the death of a neighbour's boys in a disaster. Why have we been created with tear ducts, if not to provide us with a means of the release and expression of feelings? If then, this is a human gift, why are women the major beneficiaries, at least, in this country?

The taboo extends to the decision of parents to keep their children at home during funerals of relatives. The reason often given is that it would be too upsetting for them. The real reason, if we could but be honest at this time, is that the grown-ups cannot bear the children to be witnesses to their own emotions. Let them help us; and adults will then be able to help them. How often does the fear of death derive from over-protective parents when someone dies, as well as at funerals? The body must be rushed out of the house, and only the next of kin go to view the body – and often not those either. Of course, there are no rules surrounding death, but rituals such as 'going to say goodbye to uncle', with their accompanying expressions of emotion, and often the release of tears, have proven cathartic value.

It was the obsessive Cruden, of Cruden's *Concordance*, who in the eighteenth century wrote under the article 'Tears' about the Hebrews:

> They were not of opinion that courage and greatness of soul consisted in seeming to be insensible in adversity, or in restraining their tears. It was even looked upon as a great disrespect for anyone not to be bewailed at his funeral. Job says of the wicked man, 'His widow shall not weep' (*Job 27:15*)

Sadness, like the tears which express it, may be accumulated and stored within, in the deep recesses of the self. It requires a 'trigger' to release it. That trigger may take some time to be discovered, and it usually comes as a surprise. Having kept a stiff upper lip at my father's funeral, I grieved for him ten years later, as I recount in the Introduction. That grieving immeasurably enhanced my appreciation of him and all that he had done for me.

The 'very great sadness', to which I refer above, emerged gradually, in bursts of tears over a period of years, during which the Dowland songs acted as a kind of background counterpoint, reminding me of the reality of my interior. When I finally acknowledged fully the great sadness in a nervous breakdown lasting some six months, I realized what the songs were saying and wondered that I had not heard it before. At that time, I remember being totally unable to meet people: I would cross the road rather than encounter friends, and I am normally out-going and friendly. I felt afraid in crowds and had to be led by the hand into a public concert. Getting up to speak (a rather common occurrence for a cleric) was quite out of the question. My doctor, mercifully, did not say 'Pull yourself together', but, 'This may take six months'. The detailed causes of my 'great sadness' need not concern us here: they were mainly two-fold – to do with my private life, now much healed, and to do with my professional life. The latter at that time involved counselling and caring for all sorts of people, those made redundant, the unemployed and a great struggle to establish the Carrow Hill Hostel (see chapter 5), using disabled, long-term unemployed workers under a government scheme, 'The Community Pro-gramme'.

All this intense activity brought great stress which I could not handle. I suppose I had not reached the maturity so beautifully described as seeing 'the contradiction between what we hope for and what we really are'. This phrase comes from Alan Jones' great chapter 'The Gift of Tears' in his book *Soul-Making*:[4]

> When do tears come for the attentive believer? They begin to flow at the moment when we see the contradiction between what we hope for and what we really are; when we see the deep gulf between the Love that calls us and our response to it.

The acknowledgement of the great sadness within me was facilitated not only by my previous involvement in Dowland, but also by the discovery of certain truths about the inner life.

There are jokes about the male menopause, but there is some psychological truth in it. As James Hillman writes:

> But then a man reaches thirty-five or forty, or sometimes not until near fifty, and he feels sad; there is a weight on the heart and no matter what he does it does not go away. This is typical of an anima state, an anima mood, the steady accompaniment of the soul which has become a burden, because it has not been given what it needs . . . the other aspect faces us now: the inner femininity.[5]

This feminine was externalized strongly for me by the discovery of the significance of the Blessed Virgin Mary. My church tradition has always fought shy of placing any weight on her in the divine economy, and I have been sensitive to the atmosphere of a kind of suspicious reluctance in the protestant side of the Church of England, derived no doubt from a reaction to the apparent 'excesses' of Catholic devotion to Mary. I was first drawn to the reconstructed cell of Julian of Norwich in St Julian's church, Norwich, during my enforced six months break. I discovered an old rosary I had kept in a drawer for years since finding it in a redundant church. I used it in the cell, having read Neville Ward's book.[6]

Then the reactions began. Invariably as the pictures of the joyful, sorrowful and glorious mysteries[7] arose before my mind, the tears were released. I was taken by surprise. At one point, I almost believed that the rosary I was using had magical powers. The prayers – Our Father and Hail Mary – became a repeated background, like wallpaper, to the powerful visual images of each of the mysteries. For example, the Annunciation was accompanied by mental images reminiscent of Jupiter and Io, and I was overcome by the magnitude of the grace of God being 'shrunk into a span';[8] the birth of Christ was accompanied by the groans of Mary in labour and the seraphic smile of joy at his birth when the birth struggle was over, and the miracle of birth provoked fresh tears; the presentation of the baby Jesus in the temple was a long scene, involving the conversations between Mary and Simeon and Anna the prophetess, and the sword pierced my heart too.

The sorrowful mysteries were frightening in their intensity, which was heightened by seeing Mary watching her own son suffering at the same time as I was saying the words 'blessed is the fruit of thy womb'. The horror and pain of the crucifixion seemed worse by contrast with the words of blessing. My pangs of sorrow broke out afresh at every point: the violent whipping of Christ; at the time when the crown of thorns is pushed onto his dear head and a sharp point pierces his temple; at the driving of the nails into his healing hands; when the soldiers had recovered enough energy to drive the long nail through the feet; and at the sickening jolt as the crossbeam is pushed into place. As if these realizations were not enough, my own sufferings and sense of personal inadequacy which were borne in upon me at that time of nervous breakdown caused me even greater anguish of spirit. I was relieved when there was no one else in the cell, as I did not have to conceal my tears. At the time I wondered why all this was happening. I soon found out.

It was, I now believe, the great sadness being released by one who knew the depths of sorrow: one who had watched her son all along the Via Dolorosa, falling exhausted, raised by the kindness of a stranger, then nailed to the cross, jolted upright and left to die. Our Lady of Sorrows knew. Looking back upon the breakdown from the distance of several years, this gift of tears seems like an answer to the whispered invocations, 'Holy Mary, mother of God, pray for us sinners now and at the hour of our death.' Or more particularly, an answer to the concluding prayer of the rosary, the Salve Regina, 'To thee do we cry, poor banished children of Eve; to thee do we lift up our sighs, mourning and weeping in this vale of tears.'

To pay attention to the Mother of Christ was not an end in itself: my gaze was redirected to her Son and his passion. When the tears first began, I was exhausted, spiritually, mentally and emotionally. And at that low ebb, all I could manage was to be alone, meditate, weep and be with my family, who were most understanding. Later, I realized that my so-called 'great sadness' was but a part of the tears of things, the *Lachrimae Rerum*, which are the tears for the tragic dimension of nature, for the unfulfilled possibilities, the broken egg, for lost innocence, for the child dying with the diseased brain, for the victim of Huntington's disease.

Tears are, of course, for all these things; but that should not divert us from their spiritual significance. When I first started to try and find out why it was my lot to experience this 'shaking of the foundations', I asked some holy women and men privately about it. They all insisted that it was a gift of God, and that I should not worry about it. Five years later my bishop sent me an article which astonished me:[9] it included a great list of the fathers of the church who had written of the grace of tears:

> John Climacus even considers that the tears which we shed after baptism are more powerful than baptism itself . . . Simeon the New Theologian makes an even higher concept of the baptism of tears. He sees in it the true baptism, baptism in the Spirit, of grace felt and experienced.

Issac of Nineveh suggests that tears belong between the corporeal and spiritual states. Their abundance, which marks a period of transition, lessens when one begins to arrive at the spiritual region of peace of mind, which is the prelude to the highest contemplation. Yet the spiritual masters also warn us constantly against the temptation of vainglory which can be born in tears poured out in abundance. 'Do not exalt yourself because you pour out tears in your prayer', says Mark the Hermit. Perhaps all the more reason to practise humility is that, as many writers assert with John Climacus, 'This shedding of tears (during meditation) is a sign that God has come to us without us having called him.'[10]

One of the wounded pilgrims with whom I talked about this upsetting gift was my friend Frank (of chapter 3). I should have guessed that he was no stranger to it, and he confessed to sitting through the eucharist with tears pouring down his face on occasion. He was also the instigator, in the same year of my illness, of our visit to Bobbio in Italy for a splendid interdisciplinary symposium, organized by the French scholar of Lady Julian, Roland Maisonneuve.[11] The revelation of our unitary universe, seen through the eyes of mystics and scientists, was followed by a visit to the village of San Damiano, where a humble peasant woman called Rosa Quattrini (or Mama Rosa) lived until 1981. Roland and a team of researchers have devoted

145

a book to her remarkable gifts of perception and healing,[12] and there is a sense that her holy influence lives on in the place. For, on arrival, I had retired alone to my hotel room, in the 'Pilgrim House', sat on the bed, and without warning suddenly wept – tears of gratitude, for the love of friends, for 'all this goodness that was happening to me' in this simple yet profound place. I was not surprised to learn of other friends who had similar experiences. For, the paradox is there: 'They that sow in tears shall reap in joy' (Psalm 126:9). Jesus reiterates something similar, according to St Luke: 'Blessed are ye that weep now: for ye shall laugh.'

I think this profound truth, especially dear to the Christian, is the reason why the unrelieved gloom of despair in the other two songs by Dowland, 'Sorrow, stay' and 'Flow my tears' evokes slightly less of a response in me. Yet I love both songs: they are incomparably crafted. 'Flow my tears' could so easily be the expression of the voluntarily exiled Dowland, court lutenist to the King of Denmark. 'Sorrow, stay' is indescribably profound and never fails to command total commitment. But 'I saw my Lady weep' is the masterpiece, for it has the paradox of sadness with joy in it.

> I saw my Lady weep,
>   And sorrow proud to be advanced so;
> In those fair eyes where all perfections keep,
>   Her face was full of woe,
> But such a woe (believe me) as wins more hearts
> Than mirth can do with her enticing parts.

> Sorrow was there made fair,
>   And passion wise, tears a delightful thing,
> Silence beyond all speech a wisdom rare,
>   She made her sighs to sing,
> And all things with so sweet a sadness move,
> As made my heart at once both grieve and love.

Although this is ostensibly a secular song, and the lady could be any noble (or not so noble) court attendant, yet the words allow a marian interpretation, although we have absolutely no grounds for thinking Dowland could have considered this possible. He became a Catholic briefly during a period he spent in France at seventeen years of age in 1580. But it is unlikely that he remained so, since he became court lutenist to the King of Denmark, and, for a shorter period, to the Landgrave of Hessen – both more Protestant than Elizabeth, under whom he failed, to his great chagrin, to gain employment.[13]

I venture, nevertheless, this paraphrase of the sentiments of the preceding verses:

> Our Lady stands at the foot of the cross and weeps, proud to be so 'advanced' in her sorrow for her Son. The sadness of her face draws more hearts to her, than even attractive laughter. (See the famous twelfth-century Byzantine icon of the Mother and Child, whose reproductions grace many a church.)[14]
>
> In our Lady, ugly sorrow is transformed, passion is made wise, and tears delightful. In her silent sorrow is deep wisdom,[15] and everything is given a deep movement of sweet sadness, so that our hearts grieve and love at the same time.

Fortunately, the fifteen mysteries of the rosary remind us that though there are five sorrowful mysteries, the enormous gravity of these is placed in perspective by the five Joyful and five Glorious Mysteries. Maybe this is why the shifting major and minor chords of Monteverdi's *Salve Regina* (Hail, Holy Queen), and, more than a hundred years previously written, Josquin's *Stabat Mater* (The Mother stands at the foot of the cross), are so stunning, so life affirming.[16] For the rather strange journey described above has been characterized by a sense of inner healing and strength, which continues to this day.

The gift of tears is a sign of the mending of creation.[17]

POSTSCRIPT: War, tears and soldiers

When I ran a course on preparing services for major festivals, one of my colleagues said, apropos Remembrance Day, that he hoped he would learn something that would prevent him from repeating again and again the same old simplicities in an empty fashion. So we asked ourselves the question, why do people go to Remembrance Day services? It might seem a silly question, because everyone knows the answers: to remember the dead of two world wars with thanksgiving, and to pledge ourselves to peace in honour of their sacrifice. But we found other answers as well. Some come to identify with part of our nation's history, perhaps its most glorious hour, when we had our backs to the wall, against the odds, and finally triumphed over a foe which was probably (we may say) in the grip of evil forces.

Some come to honour the flag, which means some kind of nationalism; and it may be, I suspect, that many people who do *not* come would say they feel they now belong to a wider world, our international community. They say we are all citizens of the world, and we cannot identify with a narrow jingoism. I do not believe that Remembrance Sunday is jingoistic – my country right or wrong – if it were so I would not attend either (and then there would be letters to my bishop!).

Some come because at this service they can find some solace for their unresolved grief.

> Would that my head were all water
> my eyes a fountain of tears,
> that I might weep day and night
> for my people's dead. (Jeremiah 9:1)

I want to concentrate on this last reason, because, as I spoke in the terms that follow to the old soldiers, it resonated powerfully in them.

I saw on television the reports and pictures of the very old men for whom The War was 1914–18, not 1939–45, and they were weeping, overcome by grief. I am quite sure it is possible to store up tears, unshed tears, and to become so hardened that

148

we find it very difficult to release our human emotion. Most men were brought up to consider it unmanly to shed tears.

But the grief is huge! Even I, whose war only consisted of the events recounted at the beginning of this chapter, know that. What happened to the young men? I learned from one, shortly before he died.

He joined up, aged twenty-one, and eventually found himself in Malta with a gun battery. 'Do you know what it's like', he said to me, 'to be looking up at a stick of bombs that is coming down at you? Sometimes they sent over as many as 400 planes. It was the dive bombers that were worst, because of the noise of the dive and the scream of the bomb, and you never knew whether you'd be hit.' He went on: 'The food was short – everyone went short when I left the island I was down to just over six stone.' As he remembered, the pictures in his mind still vivid, a tear stole out of his eye. I could guess what he was remembering: the others who were blown up, the ones who went ill, or who could not stand the strain and went mad, the struggle to stay alive, and the inevitable bitterness which is generated in any group that is under fire not only for months but for years. When I left him, I was curiously relieved that we had had this painful and emotional conversation. I was glad, because he had been released – just a little – from the pain and grief which he had carried those long years.

Tears are not the unmanly thing we were taught they are. It takes courage to weep. St Luke says for women *and* men, 'Blessed are you who weep now; for you will laugh' (6:21).

Let us go a little further: what were the tears of those who have had the blessed good fortune to have wept for the war(s) *for*? First, of course, they were for the tragic loss of comrades, the loss through bombing perhaps of wives, sisters, mothers; the loss in battle of husbands, brothers, fathers; and for the old man, who, hearing of his son's death in France, had a sudden heart attack – all these and many more. Let the tears roll down the cheeks. Tears will wash our eyes clean and help us see things differently; they will help us to come closer to each other.

Second, tears give us relief. What most struck me when I listened to the gunner was the sheer relentlessness of it all. The raids came in the afternoon, from just twenty miles away in Sicily, and the planes circled the island. When the sun was setting, they came in from the sun. Then they came at night too. 'When did you sleep?' I asked innocently. 'Sleep!?' came the scornful reply. 'You couldn't get any sleep. You could be six to seven days on the go.' We carry that sort of stress around in our bodies. Of course, sleep allows us (when we can get it) to lose much of the tension. But not all. Some of it is stored. Tears, unashamed crying, can release that in us. When he made us God gave us this gift of tears so that we could find peace in ourselves.

Third, tears are often tears of conscience. Men have quite often said to me, and I guess to many ministers, over a pint or in the privacy of the study, 'There were things I did during the war that I'm ashamed of.' If we will but talk of these things and allow ourselves to feel the sadness of the bad feelings, then we may allow ourselves to feel forgiven. 'I shall never forgive myself', someone may say. And of course the answer is, 'Who made you a judge over yourself? Be kind to yourself, be gentle.' The Bible says 'Love your neighbour *as yourself*', so maybe we can give our neighbour a break and care for ourselves. When a person discovers tears of conscience, they can wash him clean from the horrors both experienced and maybe caused, *and maybe caused necessarily*.

God's ancient people, the Jews, knew what they were about when they adopted the Wailing Wall in Jerusalem. Since then, many wise people and saints have taught the value of tears. One saint says, ' "Let everyone bring tears" – even the poorest and least gifted of us at least can bring tears; they have the power of resurrection.'[18]

So I am not ashamed of myself or of any person who finds the reading of names, the keening of the bugle or the skirling of the pipes too much to bear on Remembrance Sunday each year; for I shall know that they are tears of grief, tears of relief, or tears of conscience. I shall also know the truth of the words of Jesus, 'Blessed are those who mourn, for they shall be comforted' (*Matthew 5:4*). I shall also remember, 'Jesus wept'.[19]

ENDPIECE

Coming to the end of writing, we are both aware that what we have written about here is the merest, minutest fraction of a tiny drop in all the vast oceans of suffering. We have not begun to plumb the depths of the world's misery and pain. From the beginning, when we were invited to contribute to this series, we knew that this was bound to be so, so we limited ourselves to writing about only what we ourselves had experienced or been very personally involved in.

We have encountered during this year and a half an amazing generosity, both from people we already knew, and from people who were strangers, who have talked to us, come to visit us, given permission and encouragement and constructive suggestions.

This has been a tremendous bonus; these encounters have provided oases of relief and delight during a time of learning in ways we had not envisaged. We had imagined hard work in the actual labour of writing, correcting, assembling, researching and thinking. But we had not foreseen the difficulties of travelling with this subject matter in this way for eighteen months. Some of the learning has been very hard – as perhaps is only right and proper for a book which is about wrestling with suffering and death. At the end of it all we are dazed at the resources of tenacity, courage, generosity, patience and humour which have been revealed by our fellow pilgrims.

For me, becoming even a little more aware of the enormity of the sum of suffering in the world means that I am treading perilously close to the marshes of despair. Ted Wickham in his book *Church and People in an Industrial City*[1] quotes Kierkegaard's definition of faith, 'not as fair-weather sailing in the ship, not as clinging to the rock, but as swimming in the deep with 70,000 fathoms below', and I would add to this the uncertainty of whether the nearest island is within swimmable distance, and whether the sun will prove too hot, or the exposure to the icy elements too great, and whether the monsters of the deep will have me for breakfast! The claggy, boggy ground of despair can cause me to lose any perspective of faith; the sense of the numinous is lost and only the material world is left with cynical glances at Christianity and any kind of spirituality. I am travelling blind without any sense of direction.

From this angle, it seems that humankind has not learned very much. And perhaps this is the way it has always been. T. S. Eliot's line in *Burnt Norton*, that 'human kind cannot bear very much reality', is pointedly accurate. It is a relief to recall St Paul's words to the early Christians in Rome that 'the whole of creation is groaning and travailing'; that was his perception in AD 50 or so, and with the immediate access to worldwide information that we have now, we can be conscious of the groaning of the planet and its inhabitants as never before.

But there are pockets of light and humour. It was salutary the other day to remember the postcard sent to us anonymously over twenty years ago during a period of personal difficulty, which simply read 'DO NOT DESPAIR – THESE ARE DIFFICULT TIMES FOR GOD TOO' – a perspective which Hubert Richards brings out in his selected excerpts from *God's Diary*,

> 1000 B.C. (*exactly*) *15th October*
> I must some time give more thought
> to the strange phenomenon of petitionary prayer.
> It worries me.

> A.D. 1204 *18 June*
> [of the crusades]
> Western Christianity will stink
> in the nostrils of the east
> for centuries to come.

A.D. 1942 *13 July*
An outraged rabbinical court
sat in judgement on me for three days this week
before they came to a verdict.
They found me guilty.
Then they prayed.
My hands are tied.

But not my eyes.
They are like rivers.[2]

A friend who helped with one of the chapters said, 'I hope you are going to write about heaven too.' That is quite a tall order in a book on suffering and death. However, it has been referred to already in the chapter about funerals, and there are other glimpses of heaven. They come in the pockets of light and the pockets of tenderness, with affirmation, attention, intimacy, growth and fulfilment when we have eyes to perceive them. Julian of Norwich perceived the tenderness and courtesy of God for the soul, which can bring gladness and merriment, so that 'there is no pain in earth or in other place that should aggrieve us'. If we can abide with our pains and our suffering with our Lord's help and his grace,

> suddenly he shall change his Cheer to us and we shall be with him in Heaven. Betwixt that one and that other shall be no time, and then shall all be brought to joy.[3]

And we shall be oned in bliss with him.[4]

There are many passing moments when we catch glimpses of the endless bliss and joy: the helpless giggling with the delight of a young child, the laughter among friends, the wordless affectionate glances of intimacy, the scent of honeysuckle, the radiant singing of the Sanctus in Bach's B Minor Mass. Christopher Smart, for all the distortion of the religious mania which afflicted him, knew something of the wholeness and the preciousness of the created world. In his fragments, now called *Jubilate Agno* (Rejoice in the Lamb), he writes:

For the flowers have their angels, even the words of God's
Creation.
For flowers are peculiarly the poetry of Christ.

On this writing journey, there have been times of great
darkness and uncertainty, but also moments of transient, vulnerable joy and also deep delight and oneness with other fellow
pilgrims. There have been moments too which have been very
much the opposite of despair, moments of feeling very deeply
loved, described by Julian as being 'enfolded in Love'. I am
reminded of the word-picture of heaven Elisabeth Montefiore
painted in her book *Half Angels*. Talking about heaven for
children, she writes of a child dashing up to the top of the
street, where God is waiting with his face wreathed in smiles
and his arms outstretched in welcome. All the saints are leaning
out of their windows waving and cheering and shouting ecstatic
greetings over their gaily-painted window boxes full of scarlet
geraniums and sky-blue lobelias, and the child leaps, utterly
confident, into God's arms, snuggling in comfortably, feeling
instantly at home, totally loved and totally wanted.

We are interdependent with one another and both the poverty
and the riches are within. John Robinson was able to speak in
one of his last sermons of his faith that 'God is in the cancer as
in everything else'; he could say this although he knew that he
himself had contracted a terminal cancer with a prognosis of
less than six months. Julian saw in the little thing the size of a
hazelnut 'all that is made'.[5] She saw it with wonder, with the
eye of her understanding, and perceived the richness and the
overflowing abundance which is cradled in the love of God and
also the fragility and the desperate pain in the world. She saw
also that God is with us in all our woe.[6]

This was what Pierre Teilhard de Chardin was striving with
in his chapter 'The Divinisation of Our Passivities':

> When the signs of age begin to mark my body (and still
> more when they touch my mind); when the ill that is to
> diminish me or carry me off strikes from without or is
> born within me; when the painful moment comes in which
> I suddenly awaken to the fact that I am ill or growing old;

and above all at that last moment when I feel I am losing hold of myself and am absolutely passive within the hands of the great unknown forces that have formed me; in all those dark moments, O God, grant that I may understand that it is You (provided only that my faith is strong enough) who are painfully parting the fibres of my being in order to penetrate to the very marrow of my substance and bear me away within Yourself.[7]

Father, give us we pray
the faithfulness to endure
the dark uncertainty,
until the very absence of our Lord
becomes his presence:
the very substance of our suffering
becomes our joy,
and our very insecurity
becomes our confidence:
in the same Jesus Christ,
your Son, our Lord.[8]

NOTES

Introduction: Wrestling with Suffering and Death

1. Genesis 32:24–8. For the full saga of Jacob and his tribe see Genesis 25:19—49:end.
2. John Donne, 'Devotions upon Emergent Occasions XVII', John Hayward (ed), *Complete Verse and Selected Prose*, (Nonesuch 1978), p. 537.
3. Priaulx Rainier, setting for unaccompanied tenor or soprano in Cycle for Declamation (III), written for Peter Pears (Schott 1954).
4. Patric Dickinson, *A Rift in Time* (Phoenix Living Poets Series 1982).
5. *From a Monastery Cookbook*, compiled by Elise Boulding (Collins 1976).
6. Friedrich von Hügel, untraced, but quoted by Harry Williams, *The Joy of God*, (Mitchell Beazley 1979).

1: Only Connect

1. Laurens Van der Post, *The Night of the New Moon* (Penguin 1977).
2. Gerard Hughes, *Walk to Jerusalem* (Darton, Longman & Todd 1991).
3. Laurens Van der Post, op. cit.
4. Oliver Bernard, *Five Peace Poems* (Five Seasons Press 1985).
5. Eugene Provenzo, *Computer Kids* (Harvard University Press 1991).
6. Julia de Beausobre, *Creative Suffering* (SLG Press 1984, originally Dacre 1940).
7. ibid.
8. Carl Jung, *Memories, Dreams, Reflections* (Fontana 1967).
9. Laurens Van der Post, *Jung and the Story of Our Time* (Penguin 1978).
10. Jung, op. cit. p. 225.
11. Fritjof Capra, *The Tao of Physics* (Flamingo 1975).
12. Charles Causley, 'The Ballad of the Bread Man', *Let There be God*, compiled by Parker and Teskey (REP 1968).

13. H. G. Wells, *The Outline of History* (Cassell and Co. 1920), p. 531.
14. ibid.
15. From a letter written to the *Guardian* by Dr Barbara Cowie.

2: Loss of Hope

1. Genesis chapters 39, 40, 41.
2. Lawrence LeShan, *Cancer as a Turning Point* (Gateway Books 1990).
3. Bruno Bettelheim, *The Informed Heart* (Penguin 1988).
4. Cicely Saunders et al. (eds), *Hospice: the Living Idea* (Edward Arnold 1981).
5. W. H. Vanstone, *The Stature of Waiting* (Darton, Longman & Todd 1982).
6. *Church Times*, March 15th 1991.
7. Anon. The prayer is quoted in many different anthologies, e.g. Delia Smith, *Journey Into God* (Hodder & Stoughton 1988).
8. Etty Hillesum, *Etty, a diary 1941–43* (Jonathan Cape 1983).
9. Collect for the Last Sunday after Pentecost, *The Alternative Service Book 1980*.
10. Stephen Verney, *Water into Wine* (Fount Paperback 1985).
11. ibid. p. 48.
12. Romans 8:38, 39.
13. Stephen Verney, op. cit. p. 49.
14. Harry Williams, *Tensions* (Mitchell Beazley 1976).

3: The Anguish of the Mind

1. 'The Garden of Love', in William Blake, *Poems of Innocence and Experience*.
2. This church was demolished in 1981.
3. Genesis 38:9.
4. From a tribute paid to Frank Dale Sayer at his solemn requiem mass in Norwich Cathedral, Tuesday April 5th 1988, used with permission.
5. *Issues in Human Sexuality. A Statement by the House of Bishops* (Central Board of Finance of the Church of England 1991). The conclusions leave many questions to be answered, but I would like to include a brief excerpt which leaves me with hope:

> The story of the Church's attitude to homosexuals has too often been one of prejudice, ignorance and oppression. All of us need to acknowledge that, and to repent for any part we may have had in it. The Church has begun to listen to its homophile brothers and sisters, and must deepen and extend that listening, finding

through joint prayer and reflection a truer understanding and the love that casts out fear.

The statement is still a long way from the delightfully imaginative chapter 7, 'What can bishops say about gay priests?', in Jim Cotter's *Good Fruits* (Cairns Publications, 2nd edn., 1988).

6. Translated as *Christian Friendship* in 1942 (Gordon Wakefield in *Dictionary of Christian Spirituality*, SCM Press), parts of which are currently available as *The Spiritual Kiss*, compiled by Robert van de Weyer and Pat Saunders (Little Gidding Books, Marshall, Morgan and Scott, 1989).

7. Shiatzu is a form of Japanese massage.

8. Frank was the secretary of the committee which celebrated, in 1973, the 600th Anniversary of the visions of Julian of Norwich. He raised much money, organized the exhibition and edited the catalogue, and arranged the ecumenical eucharist.

4: Out of Touch

1. Anthony Storr, *Solitude* (Flamingo Fontana Paperback 1989).

2. From an article in the *Guardian*.

3. This person is now fully well and living a normal life.

4. Robert Burns, 'To a Louse'.

5. Gonville ffrench-Beytagh, *Facing Depression* (SLG Press 1978/1986).

6. David Reed, *Anna* (Penguin 1977).

7. From a poem called 'To God', in Michael Hurd, *The Ordeal of Ivor Gurney* (OUP 1978), p. 162.

8. 'The Flower', in C. A. Patrides (ed), *English Poems of George Herbert* (Everyman's University Library, Dent, 1974).

9. Schubert identified strongly with this theme, for he sets this poem to music no less then six times. Perhaps the most searingly intense version is that for the male and female voices, which he wrote two years before he died at the age of thirty-one.

10. Jim Cotter 'Good Friday Meditation', 12th April 1974, for St Mary Magdalene, Knighton, Leicester.

5: At the Bottom of the Pile

1. The state has a responsibility for homeless families, exercised through the Housing Departments of our District Councils. There is no legal responsibility for the single homeless, though money is made available through various channels.

2. See *Children of the Sun*, Morris West's account of Fr Borelli's work

in novel form (Coronet Books 1987). See also Sally Trench, *Bury me in my boots* (Hodder & Stoughton 1970).
3. Norwich Night Shelter records consistently show that over 80 per cent of the residents had previous psychiatric treatment.
4. Harry Williams, *Some Day I'll Find You* (Mitchell Beazley 1982), p. 167.
5. John Donne, 'A Hymne to God the Father', third stanza in the Nonesuch edition, edited by John Hayward (1978 impression).
6. See Julien Green, *God's Fool* (Hodder & Stoughton 1986).
7. On the Social Fund, see *Your Flexible Friend?* (Social Security Consortium 1989).

6: Sudden Death

1. Irina Ratushinskaya, *In the Beginning* (Sceptre Books 1990).
2. Nicholas Wolterstorff, *Lament for a Son* (Hodder & Stoughton 1987), p. 15.
3. ibid. pp. 57–8.
4. David Lockwood, *Love and Let Go* (Mayhew-McCrimmon 1975).
5. John V. Taylor, *Weep not for me* (WCC Risk Book Series 1986), p. 11.
6. Ursula Fleming, *Grasping the Nettle. A positive approach to pain* (Fount Paperback 1990).
7. Stephen Verney, *Water into Wine. An introduction to St John's Gospel* (Fount Paperback 1985).
8. ibid.
9. Norman Autton (ed), *From Fear to Death. Studies of suffering and wholeness* (SPCK 1971).
10. From a prayer by Alison Greenwood, quoted with permission.
11. Jean Vanier, *The Broken Body – Journey to wholeness* (Darton, Longman & Todd 1988) p. 106.

7: Funerals

1. Peter L. Berger, *The Social Reality of Religion* (Penguin 1967).
2. I am grateful to Mr Ron Carter, senior manager of the funeral department of the Leicestershire Co-Operative Society, who provided me with these statistics.
3. Jane Spottiswoode, *Undertaken with Love* (Robert Hale 1991).
4. Julien Litten, *The English Way of Death* (Robert Hale 1991).
5. There are a variety of orders of funeral service in *Funeral Services* (The Canterbury Press 1986).
6. i.e. from the Book of Common Prayer, usually the 1928 version.

7. op. cit. p. 147.

8. John Patten in *The Spectator*, as reported in the papers on 17th April 1992. It is interesting that right-wing thinkers prefer this view of reality; perhaps it provides a justification for their policies, especially policies of oppression, which depend on a lack of trust in the population.

9. See, for example, Matthew Fox, *Original Blessing* (Bear & Co, 1983).

10. Cardinal John Henry Newman, *The Dream of Gerontius*, set to music by Edward Elgar, 1900. The 1972 Decca recording conducted by Benjamin Britten has been reissued on CD, London 421 381–2.

11. Dante, *Divine Comedy*, tr., Dorothy Sayers (Penguin Classics 1955), p. 59.

12. Hebrews 11:39, 40; see also 1 Corinthians 15:22, but against this, see Matthew 24:41, 46.

13. Julian of Norwich, *Revelations of Divine Love*, edited by Roger Hudleston OSB (Burns & Oates 1952), ch. 27.

14. Robert Llewelyn, *With Pity not with Blame* (Darton, Longman & Todd 1982), especially ch. 3, 'The Wrath is not in God', a theme which the author takes up again in *Love bade me welcome* (Darton, Longman & Todd 1984). See also Richard Harries' chapter, 'On the Brink of Universalism', Robert Llewelyn (ed), *Julian, Woman of Our Day* (Darton, Longman & Todd 1985).

15. Harries, op. cit. p. 58.

16. Hymn 186, *Hymns Ancient and Modern New Standard*, tr. J. M. Neale.

17. Words derived from Psalm 44:21, and used in the traditional funeral service at the committal.

18. Jim Cotter, *Prayer at Night* (Cairns Publications 1986).

19. Raymond Moody, *Life after Life* (Bantam 1975, 1988).

20. Dr Michael B. Sabom, *Recollections of Death* (Corgi 1982).

21. Virginia Hine, *The Last Letter to the Pebble People* (University Press Santa Cruz, California 1977).

22. ibid. pp. 116, 120.

8: Past Loss

1. Harold S. Kushner, *When bad things happen to good people* (Pan 1981).

2. Quoted in John V. Taylor, *Weep not for me* (WCC Risk Series 1986).

3. Neville Ward, *Five for Sorrow, Ten for Joy* (Epworth Press 1971).

4. See *Home is where we start from. Essays by D. W. Winnicott*, compiled by Clare Winnicott, Ray Shepherd and Madeleine Davis (Penguin 1986), p. 144.

5. 'Love's Coming of Age', chapter by John Wren-Lewis, Charles Rycroft (ed), *Psychoanalysis Observed* (Pelican 1968).

6. John Vidal, *Guardian*, 26th May 1992.

7. Adam Curle, *Mystics and Militants* (Tavistock Publications 1972).
8. Von Hügel, quoted by Harry Williams, *The Joy of God* (Mitchell Beazley 1979).
9. John Robinson, 'War is not an instrument of peace', an article about the Falklands crisis, *Guardian*, May 3rd 1982.

9: The Gift of Tears

1. See his interesting book, *Music and Holiness* (Epworth Press 1964).
2. Readers may care to listen to the collected songs of Dowland, recorded by the Consort of Music. The great songs referred to here are powerfully interpreted by Nigel Roberts, tenor, with Paul Odette, on Virgin Classics, VC 7907262.
3. *The Seconde Book of Songs*, London 1600, in a modern edition by E. H. Fellowes; revised, Thurston Dart (Stainer & Bell 1968).
4. Alan Jones, *Soul-Making, the Desert Way of Spirituality* (SCM 1985).
5. James Hillman, *Insearch* (Texas, Spring Publications, 1979), pp. 104f.
6. Neville Ward, *Five for Sorrow, Ten for Joy* (Epworth Press 1971): the best book on the rosary, and, appropriately enough in this ecumenical age, by a Methodist.
7. The mysteries of the rosary are listed and explained, as is the method used, in Robert Llewelyn, *A Doorway to Silence* (Darton, Longman & Todd 1986).
8. William Fuller, 'A Divine Hymn: What is Man, Lost Man?', set by Henry Purcell, *Harmonia Sacra*.
9. 'Larmes' ('Tears'), article in *Dictionnaire de Spiritualité*, col. 287.
10. John Climacus, op. cit. Degré VII, PG88:805d.
11. Roland Maisonneuve, *L'univers visionnaire de Julian of Norwich* (O.E.I.L. 1987).
12. Roland Maisonneuve and Michel de Belsunce, *San Damiano, histoire et documents* (Téqui, with additions 1983–89).
13. See Diana Poulton, *John Dowland* (Faber & Faber 1982), pp. 26, 40–2.
14. In the Tretjakov Gallery, Moscow, allegedly about 1130.
15. Wisdom is much celebrated in the Old Testament, especially in the Septuagint, as 'Sophia' (note Santa Sophia – holy wisdom – a dedication of churches, notably that in Istanbul). This feminine principle has not been ignored in contemporary theological attempts to redress the balance in the use of gender-based imagery for God.
16. These pieces of music may be heard in excellent recordings: Monteverdi, *Salve Regina*, sung by James Bowman (ARN 68046); Josquin des Prés, *Stabat Mater* (Meridian ECD 84093).
17. Alan Jones, 'The Gift of Tears', op. cit. p. 95.
18. ibid. p. 100.
19. John 11:35 (AV). The shortest verse in the Bible.

Endpiece

1. E. R. Wickham, *Church and People in an Industrial City* (Lutterworth 1957).
2. H. J. Richards, *God's Diary* (Columba Press 1991).
3. Julian of Norwich, *Revelations of Divine Love*, edited by Dom Roger Hudlestone OSB (Burns & Oates 1957), ch. 21.
4. ibid. ch. 40.
5. ibid. ch. 5.
6. ibid. ch. 40.
7. Teilhard de Chardin, *Le Milieu Divin*, tr. Bernard Wall (Collins 1960).
8. Prayer written by Bishop John V. Taylor and offered at Launde Abbey.